Family Activities
for the
CHRISTMAS
SEASON

by Karen
Bornemann Spies

STANDARD PUBLISHING

Cincinnati, Ohio   3045

Cover photo by Robert C. Hayes

Scriptures quoted from the *International Children's Bible, New Century Version,* copyright © 1986 by Sweet Publishing, Fort Worth, Texas 76137. Used by permission.

LIBRARY OF CONGRESS
Library of Congress Cataloging-in-Publication Data

Spies, Karen Bornemann.
 Family activities for the Christmas season / by Karen Bornemann Spies.
   p.   cm.
 Summary: A collection of stories, scriptures, songs, craft projects, and recipes for use during the Christmas season.
  ISBN 0-87403-375-6
  1. Christmas—Juvenile literature. 2. Advent—Juvenile literature. 3. Family—Religious life—Juvenile literature.
[1. Christmas. 2. Advent.]   I. Title.
GT4985.5.S68 1988
249—dc19   87-18151
                                                      CIP
                                                       AC

Contents

With love and thanks

to AINA and BILL BORNEMANN, for starting me off;
to CAROLYNN SPIES, for the germ of an idea;
and to my husband, AL, for believing in me, no matter what.

Preface

A Letter to Parents

Dear Fellow Parents,

How often the Christmas season seems to be one of hustle and bustle, of concentration on *getting* instead of *giving,* of forgetting just whose birthday it is we are celebrating. How often our children ask, "How much longer until Christmas?" And how often we wish, as we answer them, that we had some better ways to help convey the true meaning of Christmas.

As my two children grew from infants to toddlers, I began searching for materials I could use to help them get ready for Jesus' birthday. Few Christian materials were available, and what existed was directed primarily toward adults.

I asked friends, relatives, and ministers what they did with their families during Advent and Christmas. I found that while many families had some meaningful traditions, most did not. And all of them felt the need for more quality time together.

Over and over again, I was reminded of how we parents are not always aware of the millions of tiny moments our children are observing and remembering. Ten years from now, we won't recall the meeting we had to rush off to or the important phone call that kept us from listening to a child's problem. But chances are, our children will, if we make a habit of it. Special family time won't just happen—it needs to be planned.

Advent is the perfect season for setting aside blocks of time to spend together as a family. As we carefully explain to our children that these times are for helping our family get ready for the Savior's birthday, we are teaching our children the priorities we are striving to meet: put Jesus first and then all else.

Family Activities For the Christmas Season describes how you and your family can plan meaningful family moments all during Advent and Christmas. Some of the suggestions are activities my family now considers to be "our traditions." Others were gleaned from families who were doing interesting things together. Still others were adapted from my reading and my years as a teacher.

Begin by making an Advent calendar and wreath. Complete directions are given in Chapter 1. Use your wreath and calendar in daily Advent devotions I've called "Family Clan Convocations." Each Convocation includes a Scripture reading, suggested hymn, and short story. One or more family activities, called "Memory Moments" (hereafter referred to as **MM**), are suggested for each day. Choose one or invent your own! Sunday devotions include larger projects and special events. Additional Convocations are provided for special days during Advent.

The book concludes with an Appendix. It gives 29 ways to say "Merry Christmas" in other languages.

My prayer is that the suggestions in this book will stimulate you and your family to use these devotions on a regular basis during Advent and Christmas. Feel free to utilize them as springboards to develop your own family traditions. (I'd love to hear about them!) But most importantly, I hope the activities you choose will bring your family closer together—closer to Christ and the true meaning of Christmas.

Chapter 1

Counting the Days

Advent is a Latin word meaning "to come." During Advent, we prepare ourselves for the coming of the Christ. Using an Advent wreath and an Advent calendar are two ways to help keep track of how many days until Jesus' birthday.

The Advent Wreath

The Advent wreath is the symbol of Jesus' coming. It is usually made of evergreen branches, which symbolize the life without end that we find in Jesus. The wreath is usually made in a circle, a shape which represents everlasting life.

The candles represent Jesus as the Light of the World. There are four along the edge of the wreath. Some people use all white or all red candles. Others use three purple candles and one pink one. Often, a single white candle, called the Christ Candle, stands in the center and is lit on Christmas Day. **Always be sure an adult is present whenever candles are lighted.**

Choose whichever arrangement best suits your preferences. As you make the wreath with your family, discuss what the evergreens, the circular shape, and the candles represent. Each of the candles has a name. These names are used as themes for the Bible and story readings for each week in Advent.

During the first week in Advent, the first candle, or Prophecy Candle, is lit. The Scripture readings for this week are all prophecies about the coming of Jesus.

Throughout the second week of Advent, the first candle plus a second candle, the Bethlehem Candle, are lit. The Scriptures for the second week are about preparing for Jesus' birth.

During the third week, a third candle is lit along with the first two. It is the Shepherds' Candle and represents the sharing of the good news of Christ's coming.

The fourth candle is the Angel Candle. It is lit along with the others during the fourth week of Advent. The Angel Candle symbolizes God's love for us and is also the candle of Christmas remembering.

Display the wreath in a prominent place in your home. Many families like to use the kitchen or dining room table. That way, they can light the wreath during meals. After dinner, they gather around the table for family devotionals.

The wreath also serves as a lovely, yet meaningful, Christmas decoration. By putting it in a central, prominent location, you witness to visitors in your home that Christ holds a prominent place in your household.

Making an Advent Wreath

Swedish Advent Wreath. Apples are traditionally used in Sweden to decorate homes at Christmastime. This wreath uses apples to hold the candles.

Materials: 4 dripless candles
4 red apples
apple corer or paring knife
paraffin and old paint brush or wilt-proofing, plant protector spray *(sold in nurseries at Christmastime to preserve evergreens)*
flexible wire
garden shears
wire cutter
evergreen branches

Remove just enough of the core of each apple so that a candle can be inserted. To keep apples from spoiling, dip each one in melted paraffin, using the brush to spread

7

the paraffin around the inner core. Or treat apples with wilt-proofing spray and let dry.

Next, wind the wire around several times to make a circle 14″ in diameter. Set the apples evenly spaced around the wreath. Fit them between the wire loops by pulling the wire apart slightly.

Clip bunches of evergreens. Twist a short piece of wire around the stems of each bunch. Attach the wire to the wreath frame, overlapping greens to make a full, bushy wreath. Bend under any exposed edges of wire.

Set the candles in their apple holders. A little melted paraffin dabbed around the edges seals the opening and holds the candle firmly in place. Display the wreath on a table, using a place mat or tablecloth underneath to protect the table surface from scratches.

Easy Advent Wreath. This wreath can be used year after year. Just put on fresh greens each Advent.

Materials: 4 dripless candles
Styrofoam ring
evergreen branches
garden shears
pinecones and bow (optional)

Push the candles gently into the Styrofoam ring, spacing them evenly. Stick bunches of evergreens into the Styrofoam until it is completely covered. Add pinecones and bow for decoration if desired.

Advent Yule Log. In England, a log rather than a circular wreath is typically used to hold the Advent candles.

Materials: 4 dripless candles
small log
drill
evergreen branches
place mat

Drill four evenly spaced holes in the log. Set the candles in the holes. Center the log on the place mat and arrange evergreen branches around it.

Making an Advent Calendar

It's hard to wait for Christmas to come. An Advent calendar helps count how many days until Christmas. At the same time, it makes a beautiful wall decoration and provides a daily way to share a Scripture about Christ's coming.

Christmas Card Calendar. For each day of Advent, this calendar has a surprise hidden behind a little window.

Materials: 2 sheets of tagboard, old Christmas cards or wrap, 25 Scripture references, scissors or X-acto knife, glue and pencil

Have the children in the family help cut 25 small Christian symbols *(stars, angels, etc.)* from old Christmas cards or wrapping paper.

Meanwhile, have an adult cut 25 windows in one of the tagboard sheets. Leave one side of each window attached to the tagboard. Lay this sheet on top of the second one. Open each window and make a small dot on the backing tagboard. Remove the window tagboard.

Glue one of the 25 Christmas card pictures on top of each dot. Glue a Scripture reference below each picture. When the glue dries, attach the window tagboard to the backing. Close and number each window.

Beginning December 1, open one window each day until Christmas. As a family, share the day's Scripture reference.

Candy Cane Calendar. This is a quick and easy calendar, one sure to please the children! All you need are candy canes in a container.

Set up your Christmas tree by the first Sunday in Advent. Purchase one candy cane for each day of Advent. Transfer them, one per day, from their storage container to the tree, as part of your family devotional. Each day, count how many canes are left to hang on the tree.

Paper Chain Calendar. Use red, green, and gold links to count the days until Christmas.

Materials: red, green, gold paper; scissors; glue; pen

Make a chain of paper links, using red and green for weekdays and gold for Sundays. Inside each link, write an activity from the Memory Moments (**MM**) listed with each daily devotion. These include ideas such as go caroling, make an ornament, have a special treat. Feel free to invent your own Memory Moments.

Each day, at the close of your devotions, one of your children removes a link, and the family does whatever it says. It helps to write down on an appointment calendar what you put on each link, so that you aren't surprised when it says something such as "Pick a Christmas tree at the cut-a-tree lot today."

Puzzle Piece Calendar. Make your own Christmas picture puzzle and add a piece to it each day during Advent.

Materials: Christmas picture, at least 8″ x 10″; piece of cardboard; glue; colored tagboard, larger than the picture; black felt-tip pen; scissors; box or bulletin board

Glue the picture to the cardboard. When dry, center it on top of the colored tagboard. Trace around it with black felt-tip pen. This becomes the frame on which you will arrange puzzle pieces.

To make the puzzle, turn over the cardboard which has the picture glued to it. Draw lines on the back to form irregular pieces, one for each day of Advent. Cut out and save the pieces in a box or pin them to a bulletin board.

Each day during Advent, pick one of the pieces to fit in the puzzle. You can even write the daily Scripture references on the back. When Christmas Day arrives, your puzzle will be completed.

Chapter 2

The Christmas Clan Convocation

A convocation is a meeting together. So let's get your clan together this Christmas. Set aside a few calm, unhurried moments each evening of Advent to light the Advent candles, sing, and read the Bible together. Ideally, the candles are lit either before or after the evening meal.

For the four Sundays in Advent, use the Sunday devotionals. Included are suggestions for an extra special family meal for each Sunday plus ideas for a family project or activity.

For the weekdays of Advent, select from the daily devotionals. Alternate readings are given for certain special days that fall on a particular date, such as St. Lucia's Day on December 13 and Christmas Eve on December 24.

As you plan your convocations, be sure each family member is involved. Preschoolers can pass out hymn books or help get materials ready. Let older children volunteer to read the stories or Scriptures (use the *International Children's Bible* if possible, since it is easier for children to read and understand). Be sure mother and dad have a part to play, too, such as explaining the Bible readings to the smaller children.

Feel free to adapt the services to meet the needs of your own special family. For example, be open to ways to incorporate any suggestions your children offer. Lengthen or shorten the convocations according to the attention span of your family members. Do as many or as few of the Memory Moments as your family wants to do. By no means feel obliged to do them all! The goal of this book is definitely *not* to increase holiday stress. Above all, have fun as a family!

First Week in Advent

God Told Us That Jesus Would Come

Sunday Convocation

The Sunday devotionals are more elaborate than the daily ones. Plan to set aside a little extra time for Sunday services and the special activities listed.

Begin by sitting as a family around your Advent wreath. Proceed with the service below, dividing up the readings among family members, if you have several who can read.

Opening Words: This is the first Sunday in Advent. Advent means coming. It is the season of thinking about the coming of Jesus to earth. He came as a little baby in the manger cradle. He came to be with us, to live with us, and to grow and develop as a person. He came to show us how to be like Him.

(Family members may wish to name some of the things they plan to do to get ready for Christmas, particularly ways that will help them to be more like Jesus.)

Lighting the First Candle: The first candle on our wreath is the Prophecy Candle. It reminds us that God told us long ago that Jesus would come. Many verses in the Old Testament tell about Christ's coming. How exciting it is that many hundreds of years ago, prophets told us about Jesus' birth! We light this Prophecy Candle to mark the beginning of Advent.

Hymn: "O Come, O Come, Emmanuel" *(Sing or play recording.)*

Scripture: Isaiah 40:3-11; Matthew 3:1-3

12

Reading:

Our Scripture reading for today talks about preparing the way for Jesus and His birth—getting ready for His birthday. All during Advent, we will be reading Scripture verses and stories that will help us get ready for Jesus' birthday. We will be doing things together as a family to help us prepare for the King's birthday. Here's our first reading.

The Legend of the Christmas Tree

Once upon a time, many hundreds of years ago, there lived a man named Wilfred, who was an English missionary. Wilfred went to Germany to spread the teachings of Christ. The people there, who lived in tribes and roamed about, had not heard about Jesus.

One Christmas Eve, Wilfred saw some people worshiping an idol, or false god, known as Thor. The worshipers were gathered near a large tree, the Oak of Geismar, preparing to sacrifice Prince Asulf to Thor. They thought if they killed the Prince, Thor would give them good weather and good crops.

Wilfred was shocked and cried out to the worshipers to stop. Dashing forward, he chopped down the oak with a single mighty stroke of his ax. From the center of the oak, there sprung a small fir tree. Wilfred explained that the fir tree was the Tree of Life, and that it stood for Christ. Then he told the worshipers all about Jesus. From that moment on, the fir tree became a symbol of Christ in all of Germany.

Prayer: Dear Lord, thank You for sending us people like Wilfred, people who stand up for Jesus. And thank You for the gift of the Christmas tree. Whenever we look at our tree, we will remember how it stands for You and Your great power. We know You can help us whenever we are in trouble. Thank You! Amen!

Memory Moment: Each day you'll find one or more of these Memory Moment ideas (identified by **MM**) at the end of your Convocation. They are all special things to do together as a family, things you'll always remember.

MM#1: Go together as a family to the Christmas tree lot and choose a tree. If possible, go to a cut-a-tree lot. On the way there, talk about this legend of the Christmas tree, what the tree stands for, and what you each like best about evergreen trees.

MM#2: Sing the German song, "O Tannenbaum," about the Christmas tree. *(The tune of this song is also used for the Maryland state song, "Maryland, My Maryland.")*

"O Tannenbaum"
(O Christmas Tree)

O Tannenbaum, O Tannenbaum,
Wie treu sind deine Blätter.
O Tannenbaum, O Tannenbaum,
Wie treu sind deine Blätter.
Du grüenst nicht nur
    zur Sommerzeit,
Nein, auch im Winter wenn
    es schneit.
O Tannenbaum, O Tannenbaum,
Wie treu sind deine Blätter.

O Christmas Tree, O Christmas Tree,
Thy leaves are so unchanging.
O Christmas Tree, O Christmas Tree
Thy leaves are so unchanging.
Not only green when summer's here,
But also when 'tis cold and clear.
O Christmas Tree, O Christmas Tree
Thy leaves are so unchanging.

MM#3: Have an All-American Meal when you get back from tree hunting. A suggested menu is:
  Red Ripple in Frosted Glasses
  Snowman Salad
  Cookie Cutter Sandwiches or
    Hot dogs roasted over the fire
  Christmas Cupcake Cones or
    Marshmallows roasted over the fire

Red Ripple in Frosted Glasses

Yield: 4 servings
Lemon juice   Confectionery sugar
1 quart vanilla ice cream   1 quart cranberry juice

Chill 4 tall glasses in the freezer. Then dip rim of each glass into a dish of lemon juice and then into a dish of confectionery sugar. Put one scoop of vanilla ice cream in each glass. Pour cranberry juice over ice cream and serve.

Snowman Salad

For each salad, you need:
3 balls of cottage cheese   Almonds
Cherries   Shredded cheese or lettuce
Raisins

Scoop out cottage cheese with an ice-cream scoop and arrange three scoops on a plate to form a snowman. Make facial features and buttons for the snowman using cherries, raisins, almonds. Shredded cheese or lettuce makes good "hair."

Cookie Cutter Sandwiches

Easy enough for toddlers to make. For each serving, you need:

2 slices bread
Assorted cold cuts and cheeses
  or tuna, chicken, or egg salad
Lettuce and condiments, as desired
Cookie cutters

Cut bread using holiday-shaped cookie cutters. Spread with tuna, egg, or chicken salad, or fill with meats and cheeses that have also been cut with cookie cutters. Makes delicious reindeer sandwiches!

Christmas Cupcake Cones

Kids of all ages eat the whole thing, cone and all!

Yield: 18–24 cupcake cones   Preheat oven: 375 degrees

Any regular cake mix   Frosting
Flat-bottomed ice-cream   Cake decorating candies
  cones

Mix batter as directed for cupcakes. Pour 3 tablespoons of batter into each cone. Fill cones no more than one-half full or they will not come out with a rounded top. Set cones in muffin tins to keep them steady while baking. Bake at 375 degrees for 15-18 minutes. Cool. Frost and decorate with candies.

* * *

The weekday devotionals which follow each Sunday convocation are shorter than those for Sundays and special days, particularly Christmas. Feel free to add additional material or reread favorite stories from other days if you desire a longer meeting time.

* * *

Monday Convocation

Lighting the First Candle: We relight this first candle, the Prophecy Candle.

Hymn: "O Come, O Come, Emmanuel" and/or "O Tannenbaum"

Scripture: Isaiah 11:1-6

Reading:　　The Backwards Christmas

Not long ago, there was a family that always decorated the outside of their house for Christmas. On the roof, they strung lights and put up huge wooden letters to spell NOEL. But one year, they got the letters backwards and spelled LEON instead. Everyone that passed by laughed at how the family had gotten Christmas backwards.

What does it mean to get Christmas backwards? Have you ever written up a Christmas list for yourself, but forgotten about a gift for Jesus? Do you worry about receiving Christmas cards from people you've left off your list? Are you afraid that someone is going to give you a bigger and better gift than you can afford to give them? That's getting Christmas backwards.

Jesus wants us to keep Christmas by *first* remembering that it is His birthday. Think of what a great gift He is to us! Can you think of ways that our family already honors Jesus on His birthday? *(Take a few moments to discuss.)*

Prayer: Dear Lord, help us to remember how to honor You. Remind us to love our family members. Help us to care for others. Help keep us from getting Christmas backwards. Amen.

Memory Moments: Choose one or do all three, if desired.

17

MM#1: Pick a Special Secret Family Pal.

Put the name of everyone in the family on separate pieces of paper. Put the pieces into a box. Have each family member draw one of the names. This person becomes his special secret family pal. The names are to be kept secret; but all during Advent, each person should do kind things for his or her pal. On Little Christmas Eve (December 23), the pals will be revealed.

MM#2: Adopt a family or grandparent for Christmas.

Find an older person who doesn't have any family nearby. Do special things for this person all during Advent, such as inviting him over for meals or helping with chores or shopping. If you prefer, adopt a needy family and do the same things. Many social service agencies have lists of families who haven't enough food or money.

MM#3: A Gift of Writing

Using one's writing talents is an excellent way to make a gift that will long be treasured. Even very young children can put this talent to use. Start planning your written gifts now. One idea could be a poem explaining how a person in your family is special to you. It needn't rhyme. It can be a collection of thoughts about this person and could even be illustrated.

Another meaningful written gift is a family history. Get family members talking, especially the oldest relatives. Record these conversations on tape. Then summarize the information and bind it in a notebook. Children too young to write can contribute by illustrating the most important moments in their lives or those of older family members.

Tuesday Convocation

Lighting the First Candle: We relight this candle, the Prophecy Candle, and remember how You have promised to come to us, Jesus.

Hymn: "O Come, O Come Emmanuel" and/or "O Tannenbaum"

Scripture: Jeremiah 23:5, 6

Reading: More Legends of the Christmas Tree
There are many other legends, or stories, about the Christmas tree. One tells how Martin Luther lit candles on an evergreen tree. He wanted to show his son how the starry heavens looked that first Christmas Eve.

Another legend tells about a child wandering, cold and hungry, in the woods. A forester found the child and took him into his home. Even though the forester was very poor, he fed the child and tucked him into a warm bed. In the morning, he found the child was the Christ child himself.

Before the Christ left the tiny cottage, He put a fir twig in the ground. He promised that it would grow into a tall tree that would bring many good things to the forester and his family.

Now these are all legends. No one knows for sure whether or not they are true. But we do know that in the nineteenth century, about 140 years ago, Christmas trees became popular in England. Queen Victoria had a German husband, Prince Albert, who missed Christmas trees after he married Victoria and moved to England. In 1841, he began the custom of decorating a large tree in Windsor Castle. Soon, the custom had spread throughout England.

German settlers who came to America brought the idea of the Christmas tree. As long ago as 1747, they decorated trees in Bethlehem, Pennsylvania. But Christmas

19

trees weren't popular with Americans until the electric light was invited. In 1895, President Grover Cleveland decorated the tree at the White House with electric lights. This idea caught on and spread across the country.

Prayer: Dear God, thank You for sending us Your Son at Christmas. We remember His birth whenever we put lights on our Christmas tree. The lights remind us of how bright the stars were the night Jesus was born. Please help us to be shining lights for Jesus. Help us to glow with His light! Amen.

MM#1: Grow a Tiny Tannenbaum

These make great gifts. You will need a medium or large pinecone, water, a small plastic container, soil, grass seed, and a small spray bottle or plant mister. Remove the stem of the pinecone, so that it can stand flat. Soak the cone in water for a few minutes. Then put it in your container and fill the container with half an inch of water. Sprinkle some soil on the pinecone. Then sprinkle grass seed as evenly as possible over the pinecone. Set it in a sunny spot. Make sure it always has water in the container. Keep the soil on the pinecone moist by spraying lightly with water from the spray bottle or plant mister. The grass will grow in about 10 to 14 days, turning your cone into a Tiny Tannenbaum. Use scissors to trim the grass!

MM#2: Family Prayer Book

Start a notebook in which you record family prayer requests and praises to God. Make bold, bright checks next to answered prayers. Add a note, if desired, to explain how the prayer was answered. Next year at this time, reread the book, enjoying and marveling again how God answered your prayers during the year.

Wednesday Convocation

Lighting the First Candle: We relight this first candle, the Prophecy Candle, and remember how You have promised to come to us, Jesus.

Hymn: "O Come, O Come, Emmanuel" and/or "O Tannenbaum"

Scripture: Isaiah 42:1-4

Reading: **The Prized Poinsettia**

The poinsettia is prized in Mexico because of this favorite legend. Long ago, in the little town of Cuernavaca, the people flocked to church on Christmas Eve. They loved to fill the Christ child's manger with flowers.

There lived in the town a boy named José, who was too poor to buy any flowers. An angel appeared to him and told him to pick some weeds from the side of the road. José did as the angel said, bringing the weeds to the church. When he put them in the manger, they changed into beautiful scarlet flowers, which Mexicans call the *Flor de la Noche Buena,* the Flower of the Holy Night.

These striking blooms caught the attention of Dr. Joel Roberts Poinsett, America's first ambassador to Mexico. Dr. Poinsett brought the plant to America and raised it in his greenhouses in Charleston, South Carolina. It was named in his honor in 1836.

There are also white and pink poinsettias. By the early 1900's, they were sold as potted plants in California. Many poinsettias are still raised there, especially for use as Christmas gifts and decorations. The city of Ventura, California, is even known as the Poinsettia City.

We don't know if the story about José and the prized poinsettia is really true. But we are thankful that God created this wonderful plant. What a blessing it is to be able to enjoy its colorful flowers in the midst of winter!

Prayer: Father God, we thank You for creating the poinsettia, the Flower of the Holy Night. How we enjoy its beauty! We are so grateful for it and all the plants and flowers You have given us. The poinsettia reminds us to thank You for giving us Your Son on that first holy night. Amen.

MM#1: Christmas Cloth

Make or buy a tablecloth for your dining table. If desired, decorate it with holiday symbols, such as the poinsettia. Put it out at the beginning of Advent. Have each friend or relative who visits during Advent and Christmas sign his or her name on the Christmas Cloth, using fabric embroidery pens. Be sure everyone in your family signs it first!

Put the Christmas Cloth out each year, so it can become a permanent part of your Christmas memories, especially as your children's signatures change. The signatures can also be embroidered with colored yarn after Christmas.

MM#2: Prayer Pictures

Draw pictures of those people for whom your family is praying. This is especially helpful for little ones who are still too young to read and write. It also helps everyone visualize the person(s) for whom you pray.

Thursday Convocation

Lighting the First Candle: We relight the first candle, the Prophecy Candle, remembering how You have promised to come to us, Jesus.

Hymn: "O Come, O Come, Emmanuel" and/or "O Tannenbaum"

Scripture: Isaiah 62:10-12; Mark 13:31, 32

Reading: Holly—the Spirit of Christ Lives Inside

In some parts of England, it is said that bees hum a carol on Christmas Day in honor of the Christ child. Holly is placed on the hives to wish the bees a Merry Christmas.

To the early Christians, holly was special in two ways. First, it was thought of as belonging to Mary, the mother of Jesus. The berries stood for the holy fire glowing inside her.

Second, early Christians also believed that Jesus' crown of thorns was woven from the holly. Its berries stood for the blood of the Savior. Legend says the berries were originally white and then turned red after Jesus was crucified.

Now, whenever we see holly, we can be reminded of three things. First, we can hum a Christmas carol in honor of Jesus, just as the bees do in England. Second, we can be like Mary, who did just what God asked her to do. Third, we can remember Jesus' crown of thorns. How thankful we are that He wore it and suffered and died to save us from our sins.

Prayer: Dear Jesus, thank You for coming at Christmas and thank You for dying for us on the cross at Easter. Whenever we see the holly and its blood-red berries, we will remember what You have done for us. Help Your

Spirit to live in us, as we remember the legend of the holly. Amen.

MM#1: Holly Place Cards

Make holly-shaped cards for your special holiday dinners. This is a unique way to remember what Jesus has done for us. You'll need red and green construction paper, 3″ by 5″ index cards, ruler, pencil, scissors, glue, and fine-point felt-tip pens.

For each card, you'll need three leaves, three berries, and one index card. Cut a leaf pattern from a green strip 3½″ long by 1″ wide. Trace and cut as many leaves as you need. From the red paper, cut a berry pattern ⅜″ in diameter. Trace and cut as many berries as you need.

To make a card, fold each index card in half. Print a Bible verse or Scripture reference on each card. Print a family member's or guest's name on a leaf, vertically, as shown. Glue the name leaf in the top corner of the folded card. Position another leaf on either side. Glue three red berries over the glued leaf ends and stand the holly cards on your table.

MM#2: Sharing Our Blessings

Give each child money to be spent entirely on people outside your family. (Our children were given $5 each last year.) The children can choose how they wish to share the money. For example, they might give it all to one organization, divide it up, or buy small gifts for other children. Nothing is to be said about the gifts until Christmas. This is to encourage cheerful, but silent, giving.

Friday Convocation

Lighting the First Candle: We relight the Prophecy Candle, in remembrance of the Old Testament prophecies of the Savior's birth.

Hymn: "O Come, O Come, Emmanuel" and/or "O Tannenbaum," or hum a carol, as the English bees do!

Scripture: Isaiah 7:14; Malachi 3:1

Reading: **The Rosemary Legend**
This legend is about the flight of the Holy Family to Egypt to escape the evil King Herod. The legend says they stopped to rest on a hillside, near a quiet stream. Here Mary washed baby Jesus' clothes. She spread his tiny garments on a sweet-smelling bush to dry.

God rewarded the sturdy bush for helping Mary and the Christ child. He called it rosemary. Then He blessed the rosemary with fragile blossoms of the same heavenly blue as Mary's cloak.

Long ago, in the Middle Ages, people spread rosemary on the floor so their houses would smell good. They also used it to decorate the altar at Christmastime. They believed it would bring special blessings and protect them against evil. Later it was used in England to give flavor to the boar's head that was served at the Christmas feast.

Today, rosemary is still used as a food flavoring. It also stands for friendship.

Rosemary reminds us of our best friend, Jesus Christ. He is the one who brings us special blessings. He is the one who protects us from evil if we keep Him in our hearts.

Prayer: Dear Jesus, rosemary stands for friendship. You are our best friend. Whenever we see the blue blossoms of the rosemary or smell its sweet fragrance, we will think of You. We know You will bless us and protect us from the devil if we always keep You in our hearts. Amen.

MM#1: Learn a new Christmas carol, such as "The Holly and the Ivy," an old English carol about holly berries and the Christ child who became our Savior. Or sing another carol about holly, such as "Deck the Halls."

MM#2: Record a tape to send to relatives whom you can't visit this Christmas.

MM#3: Make Jeweled Trees.

These attractive ornaments are a good way to recycle old jewelry. You'll need heavy cardboard, metal bottle tops, and an assortment of beads, mock pearls, or mock jewels. Equipment needed includes white glue, scissors, pencil, hole punch, and yarn or ribbon.

First, draw a Christmas tree about 5″ tall on the cardboard and cut it out. Punch a small hole at the top for hanging. Arrange and glue the bottle tops to the tree form. Fill each bottle top, one at a time, with glue. Arrange beads and pearls inside. When dry, hang with yarn or ribbon.

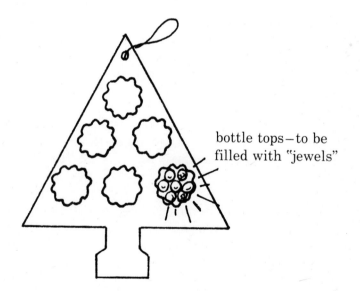

bottle tops—to be filled with "jewels"

Saturday Convocation

Lighting the First Candle: We relight the Prophecy Candle in honor of Your promised coming, dear Jesus.

Hymn: "O Tannenbaum" or your newly learned carol

Scripture: Micah 5:2-4

Reading: **The Perfect Christmas**

Once upon a time, there was a boy and a girl who saw the most wonderful, most absolutely perfect toy on television. They wanted it so badly that they could hardly wait to open their Christmas presents.

Finally, Christmas Day arrived. The children were sure their parents had gotten them that wonderful toy. One of the packages was just exactly the right size. When the children ripped off its red-foil wrapping paper, they did indeed find the wonderful, most absolutely perfect toy inside.

Before the children could play with this toy, they had one last present to open, a gift from the very old lady who lived next door. Her tiny present was wrapped in a scrap of the Sunday comics. The children ripped off the wrapping and found a glass globe with a miniature model of the manger scene inside. When they shook the globe, snowflakes floated all around the manger scene.

At last the children could play with the most wonderful, most absolutely perfect toy ever. But when they tried to operate it, they found that it didn't work nearly as well as it did on television. Its wheels didn't spin as fast nor did its bells ring as loudly.

The children set aside the most wonderful, most absolutely perfect toy. They took turns shaking the manger scene and watching the snowflakes fall on baby Jesus.

To this day, the first thing they get out when they put up the Christmas decorations is the tiny glass globe. And neither one of them can remember where they put the most wonderful, most absolutely perfect toy ever.

Prayer: Dear God, help us to remember that Your Son, Jesus, is the most wonderful, most absolutely perfect gift we can ever receive for Christmas. We can't *make* a merry Christmas. We can't *buy* a merry Christmas. Our toys will break. We won't always get the presents we want. But we can love You. We can love each other. We can't make Christmas perfect, only You can. Amen.

MM#1: Make a Snow Storm

You will need a clean, small jar *(baby food jars work well),* florist's clay, a small plastic ornament or Christmas toy, and 1 teaspoon of glitter or tiny bits of foil.

Put enough clay into the jar lid to hold the ornament or toy. Fill the jar with water to within ¼" of top. Add the glitter or foil. Screw lid on tightly. Make the "snow" swirl by turning the jar over and back.

MM#2: A Birthday Gift for Jesus

Decide as a family what you'd like to give Jesus for His birthday. Perhaps your gift will be a food donation or money contributed to world hunger relief. Perhaps you will adopt a needy family and give them gifts instead of getting so much for yourselves this Christmas. Make your decision and preparations for the gift. The gift will be given at a later time.

MM#3: Advent Scrapbook

Get a notebook with pockets and pages on which you can paste clippings. Start your own scrapbook of Advent traditions, including those ideas that are meaningful for your family.

Second Week in Advent

Christ Came to Earth

Sunday Convocation

Opening Words: This is the second Sunday in Advent. We recall that Advent means coming. We come here to create a moment of quiet in the middle of a busy day. We come to remind ourselves of what Christmas is all about. We come to light the second candle on our Advent wreath. It is the Bethlehem Candle. It shines to show us that Christ came to us in the quiet of a stable in Bethlehem.

Lighting the Second Candle: First we relight the Prophecy Candle. It reminds us that God told us long ago that Jesus would come. Next we light the Bethlehem Candle. It reminds us that Jesus came to earth, at Bethlehem, just as God promised.

Hymn: "O Little Town of Bethlehem"

Scripture: Luke 1:26-38

Reading: A Crèche for Christmas

One of the most blessed Christmas traditions is setting up a crèche ('kresh) during Advent. A crèche is a model of the scene at the manger on that first Christmas in the stable at Bethlehem. A crèche can be a small model, set up near the Christmas tree or in a special place in your home. A crèche can also be a large scene set up at church or on a lawn.

The word crèche is the French word for manger. The French word comes from the Italian word *Greccio*. Greccio was the town where the first manger scene was set up by St. Francis of Assisi, over 700 years ago, in 1223.

Before that time, many churches had built mangers. But these early mangers were covered with gold, silver, and jewels. They were much fancier than the wooden manger in which the Christ child was laid.

St. Francis wanted people to remember that Jesus was born in a humble stable. He asked a farmer friend of his to help. The farmer brought an ox, a donkey, a manger, and some straw to a nearby cave. On Christmas Eve in 1223, St. Francis and the people of Greccio met in this cave. By candlelight, they acted out the story of Jesus' birth. How wonderful that first crèche must have been!

Prayer: Dear Jesus, may we never forget that You came to us in a humble stable in Bethlehem. Your manger was made of rough wood, not precious gold. Though You are the King of kings, Your head did not wear a crown of jewels. Remind us that You, our Savior King, are more precious than any gold and jewels. Amen.

MM#1: Your Own Christmas Crèche

Plan and start your own family manger scene. Or, if you already have a treasured crèche, perhaps your children would enjoy making their own displays.

A-Frame Diorama

Materials: 10" x 18" piece of cardboard, plastic drinking straws, 3" cardboard star, aluminum foil, 4 Heart and Glitter Angels (see below)

Fold cardboard in half to form large "A." Cover the star with foil, glue it to a straw and attach it to the back of the roof peak. Glue the Heart and Glitter Angels to straws and attach one to each corner of the A-frame.

Heart and Glitter Angels

Materials: construction paper, scissors, glue, pencil, glitter, cotton balls, gummed stars

Trace around each pattern and cut out. Turn robe over and paste wings at the top. Turn these two pieces back over. Glue head at top of robe.

Glue cotton ball at top for head. Use gummed stars to make a face. Decorate angel's robe with glitter.

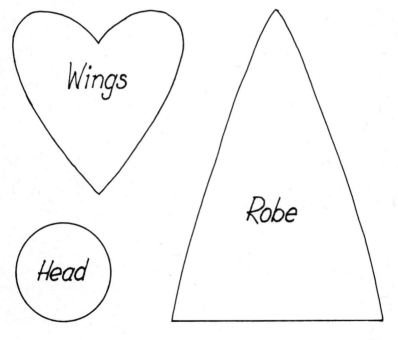

Wings

Head

Robe

Egg Carton Characters

Younger children can easily make these. Older ones can customize theirs with more decoration.

Materials: pressed cardboard egg carton cups, cotton or Styrofoam balls, whole peanut in shell, chenille wire, glue, felt and fabric scraps, construction paper scraps, yarn, scissors, tempera paint or wide felt-tip pens, paintbrushes, gummed stars, hay or straw

Baby Jesus and the Manger

Wrap yarn around a cotton ball or whole peanut, leaving some of the top free to form Jesus' face. Use gummed stars for eyes.

Cut tips off an egg cup. Paint the cup brown. When dry, fill with hay or straw. Lay baby Jesus inside.

Mary and Joseph

Cut out two egg cups. Paint Mary's body blue and Joseph's yellow. When paint dries, glue a chenille wire to the back of each figure. Bend ends around in front to form arms.

Use Styrofoam or cotton balls for heads. Attach with glue. Use gummed stars for facial features. Cut cloaks from fabric or paper scraps and glue on.

Shepherds and Angels

Make the same way as Mary and Joseph, but paint angels white and shepherds brown. Use bent chenille wires for angels' wings and shepherds' crooks.

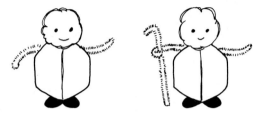

Animals

Cut tips off egg cups. Paint cups brown for cows, white for sheep. Glue cotton balls all over sheep's egg cup. Make heads from Styrofoam or cotton balls; make legs from chenille wires. Add felt scraps for tails and horns.

MM#2: Serve an Italian meal in honor of St. Francis and the first crèche. Italians celebrate Christmas with Magi cakes, fried eels, fresh melon, chicken, and pork with mustard sauce. If your family is not too crazy about fried eels, try this menu:

Grape Juice with Crazy Cubes
Personal Pizzas
Christmas Candle Salad
Crispie Rice Christmas Trees

Grape Juice with Crazy Cubes

Make ice cubes by putting a small piece of fruit in each cube section before pouring in any flavor fruit juice. When juice has frozen, put several cubes in each glass and fill glass with grape juice.

Personal Pizzas

Yield: 6–8 servings

Preheat oven to broil.

1 package English muffins
8 ounce can tomato sauce
8 ounce ball of mozzarella cheese
2 teaspoons Italian seasoning

Toppings: mushrooms, various meats, olives, pineapple

Arrange muffins on broiler pan. Spread tomato sauce to cover muffin surface. Sprinkle with Italian seasoning and top with cheese slices. Add as many toppings as each person wants. Broil until cheese melts, 1 to 2 minutes.

Christmas Candle Salad

For each serving, you need:

½ banana
1 pineapple ring
Lettuce leaf garnish

1 maraschino cherry
1 toothpick

Center pineapple ring on small plate and garnish with lettuce. Stand banana "candle" in center of ring. Attach cherry "flame" with toothpick.

Crispie Rice Christmas Trees

¼ cup margarine
4 cups small marshmallows
  (or 40 large size)
Green food coloring
4 cups crispie rice cereal

Cake decorating candies
Cherries or raisins
Small colored marsh-
  mallows
Coconut
Shortening
Waxed paper

Over low heat, melt margarine and marshmallows. Add 3–5 drops green food coloring to melting mixture. Stir in rice cereal. Let cool slightly. Grease hands with shortening to keep mixture from sticking. Shape into cones and set each cone on waxed paper. Decorate with ornaments such as candies, cherries, raisins, colored marshmallows, or coconut "snow."

Monday Convocation

Lighting the Second Candle: First, we relight the Prophecy Candle. Next we light the Bethlehem Candle, to remind us that Jesus came to us in Bethlehem that very first Christmas.

Hymn: "O Little Town of Bethlehem"

Scripture: Luke 1:46-55

Reading: **The Magnificat**

Our Bible reading for today is known as Mary's Magnificat. A magnificat praises someone or something. Mary offered her beautiful poem to God. She told Him how happy she was that the Lord had blessed her.

The angel Gabriel visited Mary to tell her about the Lord's blessing. He told her that God had a special plan for her. She would have a child. Her baby son was to be named Jesus. He would be the Savior of the world. Mary did not understand. The angel Gabriel explained that the Holy Spirit had made this possible. Mary's child was to be different from any other child who would ever be born.

Mary thought that she was just an ordinary woman. She did not understand why God chose her to do such a great thing. But she accepted God's plan. She would do what He wanted. Then she praised Him with her Magnificat.

Prayer: Dear Holy Spirit, fill us with Your power, just as You filled Mary. We know that we are just ordinary people, but that You can help us do whatever God wants us to do. Help us to see what plan God has for us this Christmas and forever. Amen.

MM#1: Write Your Own Magnificat

Share your joy and praises to God. Write a family magnificat, or let individual family members write their own. Perhaps you'll decide to make a large, framed magnificat for your home. Use the form on this page to help you get started.

OUR MAGNIFICAT

Great God,

We are thankful for _____ .

We praise You because _____

_____ .

You have done great things in our lives!

signed _____

MM#2: Work on your crèche.

MM#3: Make a Pasta Wreath

Make the wreath out of odds and ends of pasta or use popped corn.

Materials: paper plate or heavy cardboard, dry pasta or popped corn, white glue, water, bowl, paintbrush, spray paint

Cut a wreath shape from plate or cardboard. Mix equal parts white glue and water. Brush glue mixture on one section of wreath at a time. Cover glue with pasta shapes and let dry thoroughly. Spray the color you desire and hang with pride.

Tuesday Convocation

Lighting the Second Candle: First we relight the Prophecy Candle. Then we light the Bethlehem Candle, always remembering that Jesus came down from Heaven to be born in a manger in Bethlehem.

Hymn: "O Little Town of Bethlehem"

Scripture: Matthew 1:18-25

Reading: The Moravian Putz

After St. Francis made the crèche popular, it appeared in homes and churches everywhere. The Moravians, settling in towns such as Nazareth and Bethlehem, Pennsylvania, brought this custom to America in the early eighteenth century. Each family built a Christmas crib, or putz, their version of the manger scene. These putzes were large, sometimes filling a whole room. They included real lakes and waterfalls, bridges and fences, houses and gardens, as well as Mary, Joseph, and baby Jesus.

The putz was a special part of the Moravian Christmas, as was a trombone choir. According to legend, this trombone choir saved Bethlehem from an Indian attack. A large Christmas crib had been set up inside the stockaded town. Just before dawn, the trombone players went up into the bell tower to announce the birth of Christ with merry music. The Indians were hiding in the woods surrounding the town. They planned to attack at dawn— until they heard this music floating through the air. It frightened them so much that they ran right back into the forest. In the morning, the children saw their putz, all safe and sound.

To this day, evergreens and moss are gathered as a background for the putzes in each Moravian home. The Christmas Eve love feast of sugar buns is still served, and of course, the trombones still play carols.

Prayer: Dear Father God, we thank You for giving us the talents to create beautiful crèches and putzes. As we set up our manger scene and gather evergreen branches for decoration, help us to think of the very first Christmas crib. How simple and plain was the Christ child's manger. But how wonderful and special to us! Amen.

MM#1: Toy and Joy Makers

Gather up your good used toys and donate them to a toy collection center near your home.

Or plan a Gift Exchange Party. Each person brings a wrapped *used* toy. Packages are numbered. Each party guest draws a number and then claims the gift that matches. This is a good way to recycle used toys and cure some of the "greedy gimmes" that kids get at Christmastime. This works well in a preschool setting, too.

MM#2: Miniature Manger Scenes

These mini putzes make excellent gifts. Our children make them for their own rooms, too.

Materials: 3 wooden tongue depressors, 3 non-spring
type clothespins, wood shavings, toothpick,
wood glue, wire loop

Glue tongue depressors into a triangle shape. While
this dries, cut clothespins to these lengths: one 2″ tall for
Joseph, one slightly shorter for Mary, smallest one for
baby Jesus. Arrange wood shavings on the triangle base.
Glue baby Jesus on top of the shavings. Arrange Mary
and Joseph standing behind Jesus and glue securely.
Glue a toothpick at a slight angle to Joseph's body. This
represents a shepherd's crook. Attach a wire loop at the
top of the triangle if you want to hang up the manger
scene.

Wednesday Convocation

Lighting the Second Candle: Again we relight our Prophecy Candle. Then we light the Bethlehem Candle, always remembering that Christ was born in Bethlehem, in a manger.

Hymn: "Away in a Manger"

Scripture: John 1:1-4, 14

Reading: **The Ox's Cake**

St. Francis of Assisi, who gave us the first Christmas crèche, loved all animals. He wanted animals to be included in Christmas celebrations. This was because the Son of God had slept in a manger, in a stall near the animals, that first Christmas night.

Many legends are told about animals at Christmastime. One says that the humble farm animals warmed the baby Jesus that night with their breath. They gave Him His first shelter. And ever since that first Christmas, the story goes, the animals were given the gift of human speech. On one night of the year, Christmas Eve, the animals are supposed to be able to talk.

Another legend comes from Herefordshire, England. Long ago, the people celebrated Christmas with a special punch called wassail. They carried the punch bowl into the barn and drank toasts to all the animals. Then a large round cake with a hole in the center was placed on the horn of an ox. If, when he threw it off, the cake landed behind him, it was believed to bring good luck for the new year to the farmer's wife. But sometimes it landed in front of the ox; then it was thought to bring good luck to the farm's steward, or manager.

We know that animals can't really talk and that a flying ox's cake doesn't really bring good luck. But we enjoy hearing the stories of these traditions. And we, like the people of these stories, can certainly give thanks for the animals. On Christmas Eve, many people in Poland share their bread with the animals. Then they eat dinner on a table spread with wheat and straw, in memory of Jesus' birth in the stable.

Prayer: Dear God, thank You for animals. Animals were probably there at the birth of Your Son. Animals are our friends and helpers today, too. They are another wonderful part of Your creation! Amen.

MM#1: Plan to make Piroshki
Serve these Polish meat pastries at a table decorated with straw, in honor of the animals.

Piroshki

Yield: 18–24 appetizers
or 6 main dish serv-
ings

Preheat oven: 375 degrees

1 egg
1 pound ground beef
½ cup bread crumbs
¼ cup catsup
¼ cup oats
egg glaze (1 beaten egg, with
  ½ teaspoon water added)

½ teaspoon garlic powder
½ teaspoon dried oregano
½ teaspoon salt
½ teaspoon pepper
2 sheets ready-made frozen
  puff pastry dough (filo
  dough or strudel pastry
  leaves may also be used)

Thaw dough (allow extra thawing time for filo dough). Meanwhile, beat egg; then mix with other ingredients (except egg glaze) in large bowl. Chill this mixture. Place dough on lightly floured sheets of waxed paper. To make appetizers, cut dough into 3″ squares. Remove chilled meat mixture from refrigerator. Roll into walnut-sized meatballs and place on sheets of waxed paper.

Using spatula or pancake turner, lift dough squares one at a time onto ungreased baking pan. Put one meatball in the center of each square. Pull up and pinch together two opposite corners. Then pinch together the other two. Then pinch sides closed, sealing with drops of egg glaze as needed. Arrange piroshki about 2″ apart on pan and brush each with egg glaze. Bake 25 minutes, then check pastry. If it is not golden brown, bake another 5 to 10 minutes.

MM#2: Read aloud a favorite carol or a new one.

Thursday Convocation

Lighting the Second Candle: We light again the Prophecy Candle and the Bethlehem Candle. We are so glad You were born in the stable in Bethlehem, dear Jesus.

Hymn: "O Little Town of Bethlehem" or newly learned carol

Scripture: Matthew 2:1-6

Reading: **The Music of Christmas**

Advent and Christmas are filled with the music of Christmas carols. The word *carol* comes from the Greek word *choraulein.* A *choraulein* was an ancient circle dance performed to flute music. In the Middle Ages, the English combined circle dances with singing and called them *carols.* Later, the word *carol* changed from meaning a dance to meaning a song.

St. Francis of Assisi, the man who gave us the Christmas crèche, wrote beautiful Christmas hymns. The friars who worked with him also wrote carols. These carols soon spread from Italy all over Europe.

Many historians believe the first American Christmas carols were sung by the Indians. About three hundred years ago, a group of Huron Indians in Michigan became Christians. They made a manger and gathered around it, singing hymns in honor of the Christ child's birth.

Later, people gathered in Boston, Massachusetts, and Hackensack, New Jersey, to sing carols outdoors. Many drove about in four-horse wagons, singing. Others sang as they walked up and down the streets. In 1909, some people in St. Louis sang in front of each house that had a candle in the window. Today many groups of carolers sing in neighborhoods and in concerts. Singing carols is one way people of all ages can gather to bring praises to Jesus.

Prayer: Dear Jesus, we love singing to You at Christmastime, just as the angels sang to You that first Christmas. Thank You for the gift of music. Thank You for giving us voices to praise You. Thank You for coming down to us from Heaven! Amen.

MM#1: Go caroling! If the weather is too bad to go out, sing together as a family in your own home. Perhaps there is an apartment building or rest home nearby, where you could go and share the carols of Christmas with others.

MM#2: Make Cinnamon and Sugar Shakers

These are good gifts for teachers. Children can make these themselves with little parental assistance. They are also good gifts for moms, especially when given with a certificate for breakfast in bed. (Serve cinnamon toast.)

Materials: Clean baby food jar, hammer, nail, board, label or colored tape, pen, waxed paper, cinnamon and sugar mixture

Place the jar lid on top of the board. Pound five holes completely through lid. Decorate jar with tape. Write "Cinnamon and Sugar Shaker" on another piece of tape or on label and stick on to jar. Fill jar with cinnamon and sugar mixture. To keep the cinnamon and sugar from spilling out, keep a small piece of waxed paper between the lid and the sugar mixture until ready to use.

MM#3: Make Christ Crowns

On the crown below, there is a symbol that reminds us of Jesus. The letters on the crown – *IHS* – are an abbreviation for a Greek word that means Jesus. You will often see this symbol in churches. Make Christ crowns to wear or hang on your Christmas tree.

Friday Convocation

Lighting the Second Candle: We first light the Prophecy Candle and then the Bethlehem Candle. It reminds us of the Christ child who was born in Bethlehem, in a stable, just as the prophets of old had promised.

Hymn: Read aloud the words of "O Little Town of Bethlehem" or "The First Noel."

Scripture: Matthew 2:7-12

Reading: **All Wrapped Up**

The Wise-men, or Magi, brought gifts to Jesus. Throughout the ages, people have given gifts on Jesus' birthday to those they love. They do this in honor of the Christ child and also in honor of the Wise-men.

No one knows for sure when or where the tradition of wrapping gifts began. It may have been in Denmark. Danish families wrap each package so that no one can tell what is inside. A ring might be wrapped in so many boxes that the package is as big as a chest of drawers. A ball might be wrapped to look like a box of blocks. The idea is to make sure the gift is disguised!

Sometimes the Danes put a different name on each layer of paper or boxes. Then the gift must be passed on to the person whose name is on that layer. Sometimes there is no gift inside at all! There is just a card that gives a clue to the hiding place of the gift. As you can see, Danish families go to a lot of trouble to make gift wrapping exciting.

Often we, too, get all wrapped up in gift giving and gift receiving. We exhaust ourselves trying to find an extra special gift for someone. Then, if that person is not terrifically excited about our gift, we feel disappointed. We also spend a lot of time wondering what we are going to receive for Christmas. If we don't receive everything we had on our Christmas list, we feel let down.

We get too wrapped up in ourselves and forget to trust God. We forget that God has told us He will love and care for us. Instead, we worry and hurry. We hide our true feelings, just as the Danish people hide their Christmas gifts under layers and layers of paper. This Christmas, let's be like the Magi: trusting God to show us what we need to do.

Prayer: Dear God, help us to keep from getting all wrapped up in ourselves. Remind us to trust in You, to put You first. Then we will know what gifts to give others. Then we will know how to share ourselves with others. Amen.

MM#1: Family Calendar

The new year is coming. Many families like to make a calendar together, making sure each person's special days are noted on it. This can be just as much fun and as meaningful for your family if you use a purchased calendar and fill in the important dates.

MM#2: Make Gift Wrap

Save a tree: print your own gift wrap using shopping bags, newspaper, shelf paper, or wallpaper. Print on the paper using tempera paint spread on a clean kitchen sponge. Place several folded paper towels and a foam meat tray underneath to absorb excess paint. Here are two printing methods:

Gadget Printing

Print with cookie cutters or clean, dry sponges cut into holiday shapes (trace around cookie cutters or your own patterns and cut out). If you use sponges, hold each one with a clothespin as you dip it in the paint pad.

Candy Cane Prints

Draw a candy cane shape at an angle on a 5″ square of corrugated cardboard and cut out. Peel away one side of the cardboard so that the wavy side shows. Glue the cane onto a wood block or piece of Styrofoam. This will keep fingers clean while printing.

MM#3: Finish your crèche.

Saturday Convocation

Lighting the Second Candle: This is the end of the second week in Advent. Once again, we light our Prophecy Candle and our Bethlehem Candle. We rejoice that God promised to send us His Son. We celebrate Jesus' birth in a stable in Bethlehem.

Hymn: "O Little Town of Bethlehem" or your new carol

Scripture: Luke 2:1-7

Reading: A Christnacht Krippe

In much of Switzerland, a crèche is known as a *Christnacht Krippe,* or Christ-night crib. These manger scenes hold beautifully carved stained figures. The figures are carefully painted and polished until they shine.

How different these Christ-night cribs are from that very first manger. It was probably made of rough pieces of wood. It most likely stood on sturdy legs, keeping the hay off the dirty straw on the stable floor. The first manger was an ordinary feed box for the animals in the stable. Into this ordinary box, the Christ child was laid.

That might seem like a strange place to lay a baby. But actually, it was quite practical. Many of us have used a dresser drawer for a baby's bed when nothing else was available.

Jesus' simple manger bed was probably filled with dry straw, which would help keep Him warm. The straw smelled sweetly, too. Mary and Joseph could stay nearby. The animals kept Him company, also. Perhaps they even warmed Him with their breath, as legend suggests.

How like God to use a plain, ordinary, sturdy box for His own Son's bed! God always uses what is at hand to serve His purposes. This is how God uses His power to make plain, ordinary times and places and people special!

Prayer: Dear God, thank You for using a plain, ordinary thing as the bed of our King. You remind us that with Your power You can do anything! We need only listen to You and follow You. Amen.

MM#1: Make your manger a "Christ-night crib" by adding the letters *IHS* to the manger in your crèche. *IHS* is an abbreviation for a Greek word that means Jesus.

MM#2: Coupon Books

Make booklets for friends and relatives, filled with coupons which they turn in to the giver for services. Coupon books are gifts from the heart, a non-commercialized idea for gift-giving. To decide what to include in coupon books, think in terms of gifts of *time* or *skills*.

Time. Give an uninterrupted period of time to a child or another loved one. Those who are busiest may find this to be the greatest gift they could give. (You may be very surprised at your child's reaction!) Here are some possible ideas:

*"Good for one extra bedtime story!"
*"Exchange for two free hours of baby-sitting, on me!"
*"Good for one game night with Dad. You pick the board game and we'll play together!"
*"I volunteer to take out the trash for you for one week. Just name the week, Sis!"

Skills. By using a skill you have, you truly give of yourself. You can also give the skill itself by teaching it to someone else. Here are just a few possible categories you could use to design coupons:

*sewing—"Turn this in when you need a pair of pants hemmed."

*cooking–"Mom: Redeem this when you don't feel like cooking. We kids will be Chefs for the Night."

–"Exchange for a batch of home-baked cookies of your choice."

*sports–"Good for a series of juggling lessons, courtesy of your big brother!"

–"Exchange for ½ hour of playing catch."

*building–"Good for one set of bookshelves."

–"Exchange for help in building your new airplane models."

MM#3: Family Ethnic Cookbook

Each family has its favorite recipes: Grandma's giant chocolate chip-oatmeal cookies, Mother's chicken noodle soup. A Family Ethnic Cookbook is a great way to collect and treasure all these favorite recipes. As you collect recipes, note the source and the recipe's history. Group them by type or by season. They make great gifts, so you might wish to photocopy the recipes and have your children illustrate several covers.

Third Week in Advent

Sharing the News

Sunday Convocation

Opening Words: This is the third Sunday in Advent. It is time to stop and think about what the word Christmas is all about. How often we say, "I wish you a Merry Christmas!" We sing it. We say it. We print it on Christmas cards.

Why do we need to add the word "merry" to Christmas? How can we wish more for each other than the one word Christmas, all by itself? Christmas means more than making merry. Christmas is hope and faith and love and life eternal. Christmas is Christ coming. Why don't we instead say, "I wish you ... Christmas."

Lighting the Third Candle: The third candle on our wreath is the Shepherds' Candle. It reminds us to share the good news of Christ's coming, just as the shepherds did.

Hymn: "Go, Tell It on the Mountain"

Scripture: Luke 2:8-20

Reading: **The Posada**

Nine days before Christmas, every town in Mexico has a candlelight procession called *Las Posadas*. Groups of families and friends act out Mary and Joseph's search for shelter in Bethlehem. Two children lead the procession. They carry small clay models of Mary and Joseph. Other children dress as angels.

The children lead the others to the home chosen as the first *posada. Posada* means shelter or inn. Here they stop and sing the first verse of the *posada* song, begging to

52

come in and rest. From inside the house, the hosts sing the answering song. It tells them to go on their way. This is all part of the plan, though, since this back and forth asking and refusing must go on for nine nights. Then the group sings the final verse of the song. It finally reveals that Mary and Joseph are the ones seeking shelter. The door is opened immediately.

Once the group is inside, prayers are said around the *nacimiento* —the Mexican manger scene. They have refreshments. There is music and dancing. Last of all, the children are blindfolded one at a time. They take turns hitting the hanging clay or papier-mache *piñata* with a large stick. When it breaks open, candies and surprises fall out. Everyone scrambles for his share!

What a joyous celebration of Mary and Joseph's search for shelter!

Prayer: Dear God, thank You for giving Mary and Joseph a place to stay that first Christmas! How wonderful was Your plan to have baby Jesus born in a stable. We know Your plans for us are just as wonderful! Amen.

MM#1: Plan a *Posada*

Plan a *posada* in your neighborhood or at your church, or do one in your very own home, going from room to room. End the *posada* with a festive celebration, including a Mexican meal (see MM#3).

If you want to have a *piñata* for your celebration and you plan to do the celebration today, you can fill a bag or thin cardboard box with treats. Instructions for a more traditional *piñata* are given in MM#2.

MM#2: Make a *Piñata*

This *piñata* needs at least four days to dry. Materials needed are: large balloon; newspaper or a flat pack of crepe paper; liquid laundry starch; paint; string; treats, such as peanuts, raisins, pennies, stickers.

Inflate the balloon. Cut 1½″ wide strips of the paper across the grain. Dip each strip into a bowl of liquid starch. Squeeze out excess starch. Cover balloon with at least three layers of strips, leaving an opening. Let each layer dry at least partially before adding a new one. After the last layer is applied, let dry thoroughly for another 24 hours.

Then let the air out of the balloon and remove it. Paint the *piñata*, if desired. When dry, fill with treats. Attach string and hang the *piñata* with opening on top. Blindfold children one at a time and let them take turns trying to hit the *piñata* with a stick.

MM#3: Plan a Spanish or Mexican Meal. A suggested menu is:

> Sangria Lemonade
> Christmas Tree Salad
> Mexican Haystacks
> Fresh Fruit

Sangria Lemonade

Yield: 6−8 servings

3 lemons (or about ¾ cup juice)
¾ cup sugar
2 quarts water

¾ cup cranberry juice
Fresh or frozen fruit

In 2 quart container, squeeze lemons. Add sugar and water. Stir in cranberry juice. Chill. Fill glasses ⅓ full of fruit. Pour lemonade over fruit and serve with toothpick and straw.

Christmas Tree Salad

Children don't need any coaxing to try this salad – it's so much fun to pick the "ornaments" off the tree. This makes a great centerpiece.

Yield: 4 – 6 servings

Styrofoam cone
Lettuce leaves
Toothpicks
Bite-sized pieces of fruit, vegetables, cheese.

Cover cone with layers of lettuce. Fasten with toothpicks. Attach fruit, vegetable, cheese "ornaments" with toothpicks.

Mexican Haystacks

Both children and adults have fun putting together one of these.

Yield: 4 – 6 servings

1 pound ground beef	1 teaspoon chili powder
1 medium onion, chopped	1 teaspoon oregano
1 clove garlic, minced	⅓ cup uncooked rice
8 ounce can tomato sauce	1 teaspoon cumin
6 ounce can tomato paste	3 cups water

Brown beef and onions in heavy frying pan. Stir in remaining ingredients and simmer ½ hour or more.

To serve, provide corn chips and as many of the following as desired: shredded lettuce, grated cheese, chopped green onion, sliced avocado, guacamole, sour cream, sliced olives.

Each person makes his/her own haystack by first putting corn chips on the plate, then meat sauce, then layers of as many of the above toppings as are desired.

Monday Convocation

Lighting the Third Candle: The third candle on our wreath is the Shepherds' Candle. It reminds us to share the good news of Christ's coming, just as the shepherds did.

Hymn: "Go, Tell It on the Mountain"

Scripture: 1 John 4:7-11

Reading: Bright Lights and Ornaments
    Over the years, people have found many ways to decorate their homes and trees. We now use electric lights to represent the stars in the sky, instead of using candles as Martin Luther did. These lights stand for Jesus, the Light of the World. Some churches even use lighted crosses, to remind us that Jesus is the living Christ, the Light of the World.
    Here are other ways that we can decorate our trees to remind us of Jesus' birth. A shining star at the top of the tree stands for the star that led the Wise-men to the place where Jesus was. Sometimes an angel is used instead, to remind us of the angels who sang hosannas.
    Paper hearts and cornucopias, or horns of plenty, stand for the happiness that comes from giving to others. They also remind us to share the good news of Jesus' birth, as the shepherds did. Candy canes remind us of the shepherds' crooks or staffs.
    Small animals remind people of the animals at the manger. In Mexico, they are often made of tin; in Denmark, Sweden, and Norway, of straw or thin wood. In Germany, shimmery blown glass animals are popular now, but earlier, gilded pressed cardboard ornaments were used. They were called Dresdens, after the city where they were made.
    The first Christmas trees were trimmed with real fruit and flowers. Apples, a favorite of sheep and goats, stood

56

for the stable animals. Straw was also spread under the trees in honor of the stable animals. The Christmas rose was used because Jesus is known as the "fairest flower that grows" or the "Rose of Sharon."

Many of these customs continue today. Now, whenever we see any of these Christmas decorations, they will remind us of Jesus and His birth in the manger in Bethlehem.

Prayer: Dear Jesus, today we heard the story of the shepherds' visit to the manger. They were not afraid to tell others about Your birth. Help us to praise You and share You, just as the shepherds did. The ornaments and lights that we use for decorations remind us of You, too. Amen.

MM#1: Make Candy Cane Ornaments

Hang these on your tree to remind you of the shepherds' crooks. You'll need white typing paper, pencil, ruler, red crayon, scissors, and tape. Measure and cut an 8½″ square of paper. Draw red lines on it, as shown. Space them ½″ to 1″ apart. Turn the square face down. Roll the paper diagonally from A to B. Tape down the end of the paper. Curl one end of the candy cane around your finger. It's ready to hang.

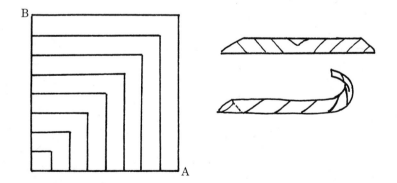

MM#2: Have everyone in the family teach someone else in the family a game, trick, or skill.

Tuesday Convocation

Lighting the Third Candle: We light again our first two candles, the Prophecy Candle and the Bethlehem Candle. Now we add the Shepherds' Candle. This week we are reminded over and over of sharing the news of the Savior's birth.

Hymn: "Go, Tell It on the Mountain"

Scripture: Isaiah 55:1-3, 6-11. Read it responsively.

Reading: **The Bells of Christmas**

Bells have been a special part of Christmas throughout the world. Hundreds of years ago, in the Middle Ages, ringing the bells on Christmas Eve was supposed to warn the devil about Jesus' birth. For one hour before midnight, the bells would toll. Then, just at midnight, the bells would ring joyously. They heralded the birth of our Savior–and the death of the devil.

But once, long, long ago, in England, all the bells were silent. No one was allowed to celebrate Christmas. At Whitby Abbey, there was a beautiful set of bells in the church tower. Each Christmas in the past, these bells had rung in celebration. But now the monks at the Abbey were ordered to sell the bells.

The bells were loaded on a ship to be taken to London. On the way there, the ship sank. But for many years after these bells were lost, the townspeople claimed they could still hear the bells. They rang on Christmas Eve– from beneath the waves.

Even without bells ringing, we know that Jesus is our Savior. No matter how bad our lives seem–no matter even if someone were to keep us from celebrating Christmas–we know that Jesus lives in our hearts.

Prayer: Dear God, we are so thankful that we are free to celebrate Jesus' birth. Each time we hear a bell ring on Christmas, it will remind us that You came to save us. Amen.

MM#1: Make Egg Carton Bells

Hang these on your tree in honor of the bells of Christmas or use them for package decorations. You'll need pressed cardboard egg cartons, scissors, white glue, paint (spray or brush tempera), newspaper, tiny metal bells and thin wire. Use sequins and/or glitter as well as scraps of rickrack or other trims for decoration.

Cut out egg cups from cartons. Spread out on newspaper and paint. When dry, decorate with glitter and other trims. Hang a bell inside each one using thin wire. Cut the wire long enough so it will also form a loop for hanging.

MM#2: Keep a hymnal in your car. Every time you drive anywhere as a family, work on learning all the verses to a carol. Good ones for this week are "Hark, the Herald Angels Sing" or "I Heard the Bells on Christmas Day."

MM#3: Continue your *posada* planning.

Wednesday Convocation

Lighting the Third Candle: First we light the Prophecy Candle and the Bethlehem Candle. Then we add the Shepherds' Candle. We want to remember to share the news of the Savior's birth, just as the shepherds did.

Hymn: "Go Tell It on the Mountain"

Scripture: John 10:1-18

Reading: Stockings and Shoes

The tradition of hanging stockings on Christmas Eve comes from an old legend about St. Nicholas. St. Nicholas, a bishop in the Greek church, lived about 300 years after Christ's birth.

Many stories were told of his kindness, such as the one about the poor man and his three daughters. The daughters could not marry because their father did not have enough gold for their dowries. One night, St. Nicholas dropped a bag full of gold down the man's chimney. It landed in one of the stockings the oldest daughter had hung up to dry. Now she could be married. The other two daughters quickly hung up stockings for St. Nicholas to fill with gold, so that they, too, could soon be married.

After a time, all children began hanging up their stockings. They hoped their stockings would be filled with gifts, too.

In some countries, children put out their shoes instead of hanging up stockings. Dutch and Belgian children put out regular shoes or wooden shoes, called *sabots,* for baby Jesus to fill.

In many countries, boys and girls expect the Three Kings to bring gifts. In Spain, Mexico, Puerto Rico, and other South American countries, children fill their shoes with hay for the Kings' camels. They put the shoes on their windowsills. In the morning, the hay is gone. Gifts are in its place.

We know these are legends. Even so, how good St. Nicholas was to help the poor man and his daughters. How nice it is of the children to put out food to share with the camels. What can we do to show each other we care?

Prayer: Dear God, the Bible story today tells about Jesus, our Good Shepherd. He cares for us, His sheep. We need only listen to His voice. He will show us what to do and how to be more caring for others, just as St. Nicholas was. Amen.

MM#1: For the Birds
String popcorn and hang on trees outdoors for the birds.

MM#2: Make Dutch Babies for Breakfast
Decide on a morning that your family would like to make them, maybe Saturday brunch. For an added touch, make name tags that look like *sabots,* or wooden shoes. If you have a pair of wooden shoes, use them for a centerpiece, filled with Christmas greens or with straw for the Three Kings' camels.

Dutch Babies

Yield: 4–6 servings   Preheat oven: 425 degrees

4 eggs   1 cup milk
1 cup flour   4 tablespoons butter
                           (½ stick)

Combine the eggs, flour, and milk in a blender to form a smooth batter. Set aside. Melt the butter in an 8″ round cake pan or quiche pan. Pour the batter on top of the melted butter and bake 20 minutes. As this dish cooks, it puffs way up. Once out of the oven, it falls. Serve with maple or fruit syrup.

Thursday Convocation

Lighting the Third Candle: Again we light the Prophecy Candle and the Bethlehem Candle. We add the Shepherds' Candle. This week we are reminded over and over of sharing the news of the Savior's birth.

Hymn: "Go, Tell It on the Mountain"

Scripture: John 14:1-13

Reading: **The First Christmas Cards**

Sending Christmas cards is a fairly new custom. It started only 150 years ago in England. British schoolboys had to write and decorate scrolls, called Christmas pieces. The boys wrote holiday messages to their parents. Then they painted borders on the scrolls.

The oldest known card was sent around 1839. It was made of paper lace and said "A Happy Christmas to My Mother Dear." Another old card was painted by a sixteen-year-old boy named William May Egley. It pictured a skating scene.

The first cards that were sold in stores were invented by Sir Henry Cole in the early 1840's. He got an artist named J.C. Horsley to design a family Christmas picture. Then Sir Henry Cole printed and sold one thousand of these cards.

The first cards reached America late in the 1800's. A printer named Louis Prang sold his first cards in 1875. His firm is the same one that still makes watercolors and paints. Prang also held contests for the best card designs.

By now, the custom of sending Christmas cards has spread all over the world. A post office clerk in Denmark thought of the idea of Christmas seals, which are sold to help others. They also brighten up the greeting card envelopes. They are one way of sharing our blessings with others.

Prayer: Dear God, our Bible verses today remind us to trust in You. There are many people in the world today who are troubled. They need to know that Jesus has saved them from their sins. Help us to share this good news with others, so that they, too, can believe in You and be saved. Amen.

MM#1: Make Christian Christmas Cards

Share the Good News with others by making cards with messages in them about Jesus. Even if each person made and sent only one, he or she would be sharing. Try designing a family card and making copies at a quick-print store. Or cut and paste pictures from recycled cards, add a verse or spiritual message, and send. Another idea is printing cards using the same techniques described for making gift wrap (see Week 2, Friday).

MM#2: Send one of your cards to someone in a hospital or rest home. Share the Good News!

Friday Convocation

Lighting the Third Candle: We light again our first two candles, the Prophecy Candle and the Bethlehem Candle. Then we light the Shepherds' Candle. It reminds us to share with others the good news of the Savior's birth.

Hymn: "Go, Tell It on the Mountain" or "O Christmas Tree"

Scripture: John 15:1-16

Reading: More About the Christmas Tree

Legends were told about the Christmas tree as early as the tenth century, over one thousand years ago. A man named Georg Jacob told a story of all the trees in the world blooming on the night Jesus was born.

From France comes a legend of the thirteenth century, over seven hundred years ago. It's about an enormous tree lit with candles, which could be seen in the forest on Christmas Eve. At the top of the tree, the Christ child rested with a halo around His head.

Another is a story about a child who wanted to be carried across a stream. The man who carried him felt the child grow heavier and heavier. Finally, he reached the other side of the river and discovered he had been carrying the Christ child. From then on, the man was called Saint Christopher, or the Christ Bearer. He was told to plant his staff in the ground. It turned into an evergreen tree like the ones used for Christmas trees.

There are many true stories about the Christmas tree, too. So many trees were cut down one year that President Theodore Roosevelt wouldn't have a tree in the White House. But his sons, Archie and Quentin, smuggled a tree into Archie's closet! Today many trees are grown on tree farms. They are plentiful, so we don't have to worry about sneaking one into our homes!

Prayer: Dear Lord, our Christmas tree is a symbol of life everlasting. You are the way we receive this life without end. Thank You for giving us the Christmas tree to remind us of Your saving power. Amen.

MM#1: Memories Scrapbook

Make a scrapbook for your natural or adopted grandparents. Include favorite drawings, school papers, and other treasures that you would like to share with those you love. Pages can be covered with clear contact paper, or use a photo album to make this scrapbook a lasting treasure from the heart.

MM#2: Start a Family Quilt

Have family members draw or embroider their self-portraits on squares of fabric. Add other pictures of the things each person likes to do. Stitch up as a quilted banner. If you add to it each year, you'll eventually have a quilt large enough for a guest bed or for use as a special tablecloth.

Saturday Convocation

Lighting the Third Candle: For the last time this week, we light the Prophecy Candle, the Bethlehem Candle, and the Shepherds' Candle. We'll go forth to share the good news of Jesus' birth.

Hymn: "Go Tell It on the Mountain"

Scripture: John 3:14-21

Reading:　　　**A Shepherd's Letter**

My dear Christian friends,

I'm Aaron, a shepherd. I watch over my sheep in the hills around Bethlehem. Let me tell you about something exciting that just happened to me and to some of my friends who also are shepherds. A few nights ago, we were sitting around the fire, talking. Suddenly, the sky all around us became as bright as day. An angel appeared. We were really frightened, but the angel told us, "Don't be afraid, because I am bringing you some good news. Today your Savior was born in David's town."

We were stunned! All our lives we had heard about the promised Savior. Could this be the day when He had arrived?

The angel told us how to find the baby. Then more angels filled the sky! How beautifully they sang! "Give glory to God in heaven, and on earth let there be peace to the people who please God."

We wanted to go to Bethlehem, to see this Savior. We left most of our sheep with one of the younger shepherds. We found baby Jesus lying in a manger. Nearby were Mary and Joseph. When we got down on our knees before the Baby, we were sure this was the Savior for whom we had waited so long!

We ran to tell our families and the other shepherds all about this Christ child. We wanted to share the good news with everyone. What a precious gift our Savior is!

Your friend in Christ,
Aaron

Prayer: Dear Jesus, the shepherds trusted in God's promises. They believed in You. They shared their faith with others. Help us to be like them. Amen.

MM#1: Work on your family quilt.

MM#2: Make Edible Cookie Dough Ornaments

Yield: 5 dozen 2½″ cookie ornaments
Preheat oven: 350 degrees

2 cups butter or margarine, softened	Food coloring
	Plastic wrap
2¼ cups sifted powdered sugar	Rolling pin and cloth
	Cookie cutters
6 hard-boiled eggs	Cookie sheets
2 teaspoons cream of tartar	Skewer or chopstick
2 teaspoons baking soda	Thread
2 teaspoons almond extract	
5 cups unbleached flour	

Cream butter and sugar until light and fluffy. Remove yolks from hard-boiled eggs. Mash just the yolks and add to butter/sugar mixture. Add cream of tartar, baking soda, and almond extract, beating well. Gradually add flour, mixing well after each addition. Divide dough into four equal amounts. Leave one plain. Add one color each to the other portions. Wrap each separately in plastic wrap. Chill at least 1 hour.

Roll dough out to ¼″ thickness on lightly floured board. Cut with cookie cutters. Use the dough scraps to make facial features and other decorations. Make a hole at top of each cookie, using a skewer or chopstick. Transfer cookie to ungreased cookie sheet.

Bake at 350 degrees for 8 to 10 minutes. Cool on baking sheets for 1 to 2 minutes before removing to racks. Holes can be repunched at this time if necessary. Cool completely, then hang. Be sure to "test" a few—they're delicious!

Fourth Week in Advent

Jesus Is Coming Again

Sunday Convocation

Opening Words: Christmas would not mean much if we worshiped at the Christ child's crib – and then went back to being the same old person. Christmas should change us – renew us. If we're new on the inside, we want to help all of God's children. We want to help those who are hungry or lonely or need a friend. We don't have to go to a far country to do this. We can share God's love with the people we meet at the store, at school, or at work. *(Family members may wish to share ways that Jesus is working in their lives to make them feel loved and ways that they are sharing the love of Christ with others.)*

Lighting the Fourth Candle: On this fourth Sunday in Advent, we light our first three candles. Then we add the Angel Candle to remind us to be like angels, sharing God's love.

Hymn: "Hark, the Herald Angels Sing"

Scripture: Acts 1:1, 2, 4-11

Reading: **The Gentle Camel of Jesus**

Legends tell us that long, long ago in the Middle East, there lived three Wise-men: Caspar of Tarsus, Melchior of Arabia, and Balthasar of Saba. Caspar, Melchior, and Balthasar probably lived in an area where Syria and Lebanon are today. The Magi, as the Wise-men are also called, were part of a group of men who spent their whole lives studying the stars.

Many children who live in the Middle East believe a legend about the Gentle Camel of Jesus. This camel was

68

supposed to be the youngest of the three camels which brought the Magi to Bethlehem. The poor camel was so tired at the end of the long journey that it lay down and cried outside the stable door. When baby Jesus heard the camel's cries, He lifted His tiny hand. He blessed the beast with happiness and eternal life.

This is why some children sing to the camel and ask him to bring presents to them, just as he took presents to Jesus. The children leave a dish of water and a bowl of wheat for the camel. The animal is said to leave toys and candies for good boys and girls. Those who have been naughty find only a black mark on their wrists when they wake up in the morning.

Prayer: Dear Jesus, we enjoy hearing stories from all over the world. We know these are made-up tales. The story that never changes is the story about You and Your birth. You are with us always. We thank You we can believe in You. Amen.

MM#1: Plan a Menu from the Middle East.

Included are a not-too-spicy main dish plus a beverage and dessert featuring two commonly used Middle Eastern foods—yogurt and dates. Suggested menu:
Yogurt Milkshakes
Pita Pockets
Christmas Date-Nut Cake

Yogurt Milkshakes

For each serving, you need:
1 cup yogurt (any flavor)
½ cup milk
1 egg
1 scoop ice cream

1 teaspoon almond or vanilla extract
1 cup fresh or frozen fruit

Mix yogurt, milk, egg, flavoring, and fruit in blender. Pour into a tall glass over the scoop of ice cream.

Pita Pockets

Family members can create their own variations of this dish. It can even be served for breakfast, filled with scrambled eggs.

Yield: 6–8 servings   Preheat oven: 300 degrees

1 package of pita bread
Various fillings: Taco (ground beef/tomato sauce/onion)
                Scrambled eggs and cheese
                Tuna salad
                Sliced cold cuts and cheese

Optional toppers to add to any filling:
1 teaspoon sunflower seeds   Sliced avocado
1 tablespoon grated carrots   Chopped cucumbers or
1 tablespoon raisins   tomato
1 tablespoon chopped celery   Sprouts or shredded
   or apple   lettuce
2 tablespoons grated cheese

Christmas Date-Nut Cake

Yield: one 8″ or 9″ cake   Preheat oven: 350 degrees

1 cup chopped dates   1 cup boiling water
½ cup chopped walnuts   2 tablespoons butter
½ cup sugar   1 teaspoon vanilla
1¼ cup flour   Whipped cream topping
1 teaspoon baking powder

In a large bowl, mix dates, walnuts, and dry ingredients. In a smaller bowl, combine water, butter, and vanilla. Add this to date/nut mixture and stir until all ingredients are moistened. Bake in greased and floured 8″ or 9″ square pan at 350 degrees for 35 to 40 minutes. Serve warm, topped with whipped cream topping.

MM#2: Start a Christmas Play

Plan a family Christmas puppet play, using stick, fabric, or finger puppets. Write your own or use a library book version, such as Tomie de Paola's excellent *The Christmas Pageant.* Plan to perform it on Christmas Day.

MM#3: Make Pinecone Trees

These make good use of old jewelry and are wonderful centerpieces, if you glue a circle of felt to the bottom.

Materials: Pinecones, beads, mock pearls, mock jewels, large sequins (round or star-shaped), white glue, toothpicks, felt for centerpiece base

Glue beads at the tips of the pinecone to represent tree ornaments. Use sequins for "lights" or the star at the top of the tree. Use toothpicks to help position beads and sequins. When dry, add the felt circle to the bottom.

Monday Convocation

Lighting the Fourth Candle: Now we light four candles: the Prophecy Candle, the Bethlehem Candle, the Shepherds' Candle, and finally the Angel Candle. They remind us that God promised that Jesus will come again, to take us to Heaven with Him.

Hymn: "Hark, the Herald Angels Sing" or listen to a record of carols.

Scripture: Matthew 25:1-13

Reading: **The Magic Mule**

Today, we have another legend from the Middle East. It is about the Magic Mule. Many Lebanese children believe that the Magic Mule brings gifts after Christmas. This belief came from an old legend about a man who was traveling the countryside by mule. At midnight, he tied the animal to a tree and went to a village nearby. When he came back, the mule was not there. Then he heard braying. He looked up and saw his mule thrashing around up in the branches of the tree.

The trees in that area were believed to bow at midnight, in honor of Jesus. They also bowed to warn the Magi that they should not return to Herod. Herod was an evil king who wanted to kill Jesus. The bowing trees pointed the safe way for the Magi to return home.

Now the man understood what had happened to his mule. At midnight, the tree bent in honor of the Christ child. When the branches bent back, they caught the mule. They carried him to the top of the tree.

Since that time, the mule has been considered magical. That is why children leave their doors open on Epiphany Eve (January 5). They are waiting for the Magic Mule to bring them gifts, just as the Three Kings brought gifts to

Jesus. The Magic Mule arrives exactly at twelve. The children try to stay awake to see him, but they never can.

Prayer: Dear Jesus, You are the best gift we could ever have. Teach us to treasure You more than any other gift. Amen.

MM#1: You Are a Gift!
Have each person in the family draw a picture of a special gift he has given or received. Then have each person draw a picture of himself. Talk about ways each person in the family is a gift to family and friends. Have each family member share one way each other family member is special to him. Record this on each person's picture. Display the pictures.

MM#2: Learn to say "Merry Christmas" in another language. *(See Appendix.)*

Tuesday Convocation

Lighting the Fourth Candle: After we light the Prophecy Candle, the Bethlehem Candle, and the Shepherds' Candle, we light our Angel Candle. It reminds us that Jesus is coming again.

Hymn: "Hark, the Herald Angels Sing" or read the words aloud to "Angels We Have Heard on High"

Scripture: Matthew 25:31-46

Reading: Dip-in-the-Pot

Sweden is a country with many rich Christmas traditions, such as St. Lucia's Day on December 13. Another interesting tradition concerns trolls. Long ago, the Swedes believed trolls searched for dark corners in which to hide. Then they could sneak out and do their bad deeds without being seen. Thus, a custom developed in Sweden that each family made sure its home was very, very clean. At Christmastime, every corner and every cupboard would be made spotless.

Swedes are also known for their excellent foods and desserts. On Christmas Eve, the Swedes have a special tradition at noonday. Everyone gathers in the kitchen to sample *doppa i grytan,* or "dip-in-the-pot." A huge kettle of broth simmers on the stove. Each member dips a piece of special rye bread in the pot. As they eat their bread, the family members are reminded that all food is precious. No matter how simple the food, the Swedes give thanks for it.

Prayer: Dear Father, we have so many blessings. We have more than enough food to eat, sometimes we forget to be truly thankful for it. Instead, we complain about having to eat our vegetables or to try a new dish. Help each of us to remember, as the Swedes do, that all food is precious. Amen.

MM#1: Dip-in-the-Pot

Make your own Pot of Blessings. Have each family member write down or color a picture of something for which he is thankful. Encourage family members to think of things that others in the family have done for them. Put all the messages in a big pot. Pull them out one at a time and share them with the whole family.

MM#2: Work on your family quilt.

MM#3: Make a Christmas Card Church

Fill this church with cookies to make a delicious gift for a teacher, friend, or special relative. You'll need a pencil, ruler, hole punch, and scissors. Materials required are construction paper, 7 Christmas cards (new or used), yarn, and foil.

First make your patterns. On the construction paper, draw a 4″ square. Cut it out. This is Pattern A.

Measure and cut out a rectangle that is 4″ x 7″. Put a dot 4″ up each side and in the middle of the top. Draw lines between these dots, as shown, and cut to form Pattern B.

Measure and cut out a 3″ square. Round off the top and save. This will be the church door. Draw and cut out a cross.

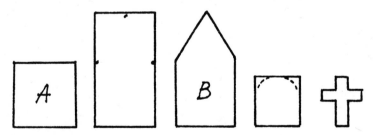

Place Pattern A on a Christmas card. Trace around it and cut out. Repeat with additional cards until you have five pieces. Place Pattern B on a card. Trace around it and cut out. Repeat. Then punch holes in all seven cards, as shown.

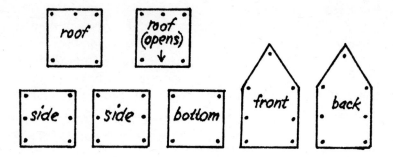

Tie shapes together with yarn. Glue cross and door to one of the pointed sections. Line church with foil and fill with cookies.

Wednesday Convocation

Lighting the Fourth Candle: We light our first three candles. Then we light the Angel Candle, which fills us with Your light, Lord Jesus.

Hymn: "Hark, the Herald Angels Sing"

Scripture: 1 Thessalonians 4:13-18

Reading: **Another Nazareth**

We've already heard about Nazareth, Pennsylvania, where the Moravians live. In the Texas Panhandle, there is another town called Nazareth, also named after the town where Jesus lived. It's a quiet, ordinary town, just as Jesus' hometown was. It lies on the flat plains. Acres of grain grow here. Sheep graze in nearby fields. Farmers and carpenters live there, just as they did in the Nazareth of Jesus' day.

It's also a small town, just as Jesus' Nazareth was. Less than 300 people live there. Many have lived there all their lives, just as people did in Jesus' day. In Bible times, people did not move as much as they do now. Often, they would live in the same place where their grandparents and great-grandparents had lived.

But Nazareth, Texas, is different from Jesus' Nazareth. It has a variety store and a volunteer fire department. It doesn't have camels—but sometimes people ride on horseback into town.

In front of a few houses are small shrines. They hold statues of Mary and baby Jesus. Perhaps the people want to show that Nazareth, Texas, is like that first Nazareth.

And so it is, even though the people in Nazareth, Texas, drive cars and have electricity and other things Jesus did not have, it is an ordinary town. God uses ordinary towns, like the Nazareth where Mary and Joseph lived. God uses ordinary people, like Mary, like Joseph, like you and me.

Prayer: Dear God, we are ordinary people. But we know that if we trust in You, we can do extraordinary things. Whatever You need done, we can do—if we put our faith and trust in You. Amen.

MM#1: Practice your Family Puppet Play.

MM#2: Plan a Cookie Exchange

Arrange with several families to do a cookie exchange. Each family brings three dozen cookies, plus a few extras (for tasting). The cookies are placed on trays, with the extras in a different place. Each family chooses from the displayed cookies, filling their container with three dozen cookies. This is a great way to have a variety of Christmas cookies, without having to bake several different batches. The extras are eaten right there at the cookie exchange party!

MM#3: Make a Chain of Angels

In honor of the Angel Candle, fold and cut a paper doll-type chain for your tree. First, cut strips of paper 3½" x 20" (or longer, if you have larger sheets of paper). Fold the paper accordion style, each fold being 3½" wide. You should end up with a folded 3½" square. Enlarge the pattern shown here to 3½". Center the pattern on the paper, trace and cut out. Join several chains with yarn loops or tape. Decorate the angels with glitter, rickrack or other trims.

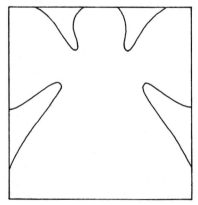

Thursday Convocation

Lighting the Fourth Candle: We light our Prophecy Candle, our Bethlehem Candle, our Shepherds' Candle, and finally, our Angel Candle. Their shining lights remind us to be shining lights for Jesus.

Hymn: Read a carol aloud.

Scripture: 1 Thessalonians 5:1-10

Reading: Mince Pie—The Spirit of Humility
Mincemeat pies are an important part of many Christmas celebrations, especially in England. In ancient times, they were made in rectangular shapes. This stood for the manger. They were filled with eastern spices to represent the gifts of the Wise-men. Each pie was a reminder of the humble birth of our Savior, in a poor manger. Pies made in this shape were easy to form. Then they were laid on the flat stone floors of the baking ovens.

People believed that eating a piece of mincemeat pie would bring good luck. Each piece would bring one day of happiness. Or, if a person ate a pie at twelve houses, he was supposed to have good luck for the next twelve months. For these reasons large pies were put on tables for visitors to serve themselves.

Then the Puritan ruler, Oliver Cromwell, came to power in 1653. He did not want the people to celebrate at Christmastime. There was to be no gift giving or feasting or celebrating with any of the old customs. No one was allowed to make and serve the rectangular mince pies. So housewives changed and baked their pies in round metal pans instead.

Prayer: Dear God, we know You want us to celebrate the birth of Your Son. Let us use gift giving and feasting to remind us of Jesus' birth. Keep us from using our celebrating to be greedy. Amen.

MM#1: Make Mini Mince Pies

Mincemeat pies have been a tradition in England for centuries. In Victorian times, when mother was baking these pies, she would break off bits of dough and give the children scoops of mincemeat so they could make their own small turnovers.

Yield: 4–8 servings   Preheat oven: 400 degrees

2 sheets ready-made frozen puff pastry dough (filo dough or strudle pastry leaves may also be used)
12 ounce jar of mincemeat
1 egg for glaze

Thaw dough and cut each sheet into four squares. Allow extra time for thawing filo dough. Spoon on filling. Fold over edges to form triangle and seal by pressing down with fork tines. Brush with egg glaze (beat egg, add 1 teaspoon water). Bake on greased cookie sheets for 10-15 minutes, until golden brown.

MM#2: Birthday Gift for Jesus

Back in the first week of Advent (Saturday), we talked about planning a birthday gift for Jesus. If you've already decided on one, now is a good time to give it to the recipient. If you haven't done anything on this yet, but would like to, reread that Memory Moment.

Friday Convocation

Lighting the Fourth Candle: We light again our four weekly Advent candles. Let us especially be reminded by the Angel Candle to sing God's praises.

Hymn: "Hark, the Herald Angels Sing" or "This Little Christian Light of Mine"

Scripture: John 14:1-4, John 8:12

Reading: Luminaries — Jesus, the Light of the World

Our Bible verses today talk about trusting in Jesus, our Light of the World. Trusting in Jesus means talking to Jesus about everything in our lives. When we want to know what to do next, we need to ask Jesus. When we want to know what to say, we need to ask Jesus. If someone is unfriendly to us, we need to ask Jesus to show us how to love this person. When we act this way, we shine with Christ's light.

At Christmastime, we use lots of lights and candles. They stand for this Christian light. Luminaries are a very special way to have the outside of your home glow with such light.

To make luminaries, use medium-sized brown paper bags. Draw a simple design, such as a star or Christmas tree, on the bags. Use a paper punch to punch holes along the lines.

Fill the bags with about two inches of sand. Place a small votive candle in the bottom. When it is lit, the flickering candle shines through the design you have cut.

These are lovely to put out when you are expecting company or having a party, such as a cookie exchange or a *posada*. Everyone who sees them asks what they are. Then you have a perfect chance to tell about how your luminaries shine in honor of Jesus, our Light of the World.

Prayer: Dear Jesus, let our actions show that we are lights for You. If we always try to act like Christian lights, we will be ready for You when You come again. Amen.

MM#1: Make luminaries.

MM#2: Practice Your Family Puppet Play.

MM#3: Make Overlapping Stars

Let your light shine with these quick and easy tree ornaments. They can also be used for gift tags.

Materials: construction paper, gummed stars, scissors, pencil, stapler, hole punch, and thread.

Trace around the three inch pattern. Then make a star that is four inches and one that is five inches. Use a different color for each star. Lay them on top of each other, placing largest star on bottom. Staple together in center. Stick gummed star on top of staple to hide it. Punch hole in one tip of largest star and hang with thread loop.

Saturday Convocation

Lighting the Angel Candle: This is the last day of the fourth week in Advent. We light our four candles. We wait now for Your coming, Jesus.

Hymn: "Hark, the Herald Angels Sing"

Scripture: Isaiah 25:9; Matthew 5:14-16

Reading: **The Son and the Sun**

The sun is used as a symbol to tell us that Jesus is coming. You will see it on banners in many churches. Sometimes altar cloths and the robes that ministers or priests wear will have a sun embroidered on them, too.

Often, the sun will have the letters *IHS* on it. If you remember, these letters are an abbreviation of the Greek word that means Jesus. You will see these letters used quite often in church decorations. We used them on our crowns (Advent, Week 2, Thursday).

Think back to Mary's Magnificat and God's promises to Mary. He said He would send a son, to be our Savior. This word son sounds just like the sun in the sky. But it is spelled differently. We often use a picture of the sun to stand for Jesus, the Son of God. We have also talked about Jesus as the Light of the World. The sun shines in the sky, giving us light. Jesus, the Son of God, shines throughout Heaven and earth.

Whenever we see the sun, we can remember that God keeps His promises to us. He sent us His Son.

Prayer: Dear God, thank You for giving us Your only Son to be our Savior. Thank You for giving us the sun to shine in the sky. It reminds us that You keep Your promises. The sun reminds us of the Son. Amen.

MM#1: Make a Son/Sun Symbol

Cut out a sun from construction paper or felt. Print the letters *IHS* on it and hang it proudly. Or make several small ones, to use for Christmas tree decorations.

MM#2: Turn on only your Christmas tree lights and have each family member share a favorite Christmas memory.

Convocations for Special Days

Use these convocations as desired on the special days noted below. They include alternative readings for December 5, St. Nicholas Eve; December 13, St. Lucia's Day, which is celebrated in Swedish households; and December 23, Little Christmas Eve, celebrated in Denmark. Special convocations are also provided for Christmas Eve and Christmas Day.

December 5 — St. Nicholas Eve

Lighting the Advent Candles: Light the appropriate number of Advent candles, depending on whether December 5 falls in the first or second week of Advent. Then say: "We light these candles in special honor of St. Nicholas Eve."

Hymn: Listen to a record of carols.

Scripture: Matthew 22:35-40

Reading: St. Nicholas and Black Peter

In the Netherlands, the Christmas season begins on December 5, St. Nicholas Eve. St. Nicholas, who was a bishop in the early Greek church, was always ready to help those in need. It is thought that the custom of giving gifts to children in his name began about six hundred years ago. Nuns would leave presents at the homes of the poor on the eve of St. Nicholas Day. This custom spread across Europe, until the night became one of great celebration. It includes street parades led by someone dressed as St. Nicholas, riding a white horse.

Gradually this custom became connected with parents trying to get their children to behave better. Good St.

84

Nicholas was said to visit every home to find out which children were good all year. The story goes that he and his helper, Black Peter, journeyed to Amsterdam from Spain, visiting every home. This part of the legend probably comes from the time when the Dutch people were ruled by Spain.

St. Nicholas wears a white robe with a red cassock over it. A cassock is an ankle-length garment with close-fitting sleeves worn by priests. St. Nicholas also wears a tall headdress and carries a golden shepherd's crook. His beard is long and white.

Black Peter slips down each chimney, since St. Nicholas must not get his white robe dirty. Peter puts presents in the wooden shoes which the children have placed by the chimney. But first, he removes the offerings the children have left for St. Nicholas' white horse, gifts such as a lump of sugar or a carrot or some bits of hay.

Black Peter leaves many fine treats for the children, including pink and white candy hearts or marzipan candy shaped like apples, potatoes, or tiny fat pigs. But best of all, he leaves large gingerbread figures of St. Nicholas on his horse or Black Peter with his bag of treats.

Prayer: Dear Father in Heaven, we enjoy listening to the stories of how people in other lands celebrate Christmas. It helps us to understand these people, such as the children in the Netherlands. But let us always remember that the true story of Christmas is the story of the birth of Your Son. Amen.

MM#1: Be a St. Nicholas
Talk about ways to share something with someone this week. The sharing or the kind action should be done in secret, so that no one knows the identity of the giver.

MM#2: Make Gingerbread Figures
Make figures like the ones left by Black Peter.

Olive's Gingerbread People

Yield: 2½ dozen cookies   Preheat oven: 350 degrees

1 cup dark molasses
1 cup sugar
1 cup shortening
2 eggs
5 cups flour
2 teaspoons soda dissolved in ¼ cup sour milk

1 teaspoon salt
1 tablespoon ground ginger
1 tablespoon ground cinnamon
½ teaspoon nutmeg
¼ teaspoon allspice
½ teaspoon cloves
Decorating candies and icing

Mix molasses, sugar, and shortening. Stir in eggs. Mix in remaining ingredients except icing and candies. Cover and chill at least 2 hours.

Preheat oven to 350 degrees. Roll dough ¼" thick on floured board. Cut with floured cookie cutters. Decorate with raisins and candies, if desired. Place 2" apart on lightly greased cookie sheet. Bake until no indentation remains when you touch cookies, about 10 minutes. Cool and decorate with St. Nicholas Icing, if desired.

St. Nicholas Icing

2 tablespoons butter
2 tablespoons powdered sugar

1 teaspoon vanilla extract
2-3 tablespoons milk
Food coloring

Melt butter and set aside. Sift sugar into medium bowl. Add butter, vanilla, and milk. Beat until smooth. Frosting should be of easy spreading consistency. (Add a few more drops of milk or spoonful of sugar if necessary.) Divide icing into cups and color each one with a few drops of different food coloring. Spread icing onto cookies or use in decorating tubes.

MM#3: Cut out pink and white paper hearts and hang them on your Christmas tree, as reminders of the kind things that St. Nicholas did for others.

December 13 — St. Lucia's Day

Lighting the Advent Candles: Again, light the appropriate number of Advent candles, depending on the week in which December 13 falls. Then say: "Today is St. Lucia's Day. Lucia means light. How fitting that we should light candles on this festive day."

Hymn: "I Am So Glad Each Christmas Eve"

Scripture: Romans 5:1-5, 8-11

Reading: Luciadagen

In Sweden, December 13 is *Luciadagen,* or St. Lucia's Day. It is the beginning of their holiday season. St. Lucia was a young woman who lived many centuries ago in Rome. She was a Christian and would not give up her faith to marry a pagan unbeliever. She was tortured and killed by order of the Roman Emperor, Diocletian.

Stories of her courage were brought to Sweden by missionaries. She became known as the Lucia Bride. Old people said the Lucia Bride would go out early in the morning to bring food and drink to the poor. She wore white robes and a crown of light.

This story is acted out in Swedish homes. The oldest daughter is the Lucia Bride. Early in the morning on December 13, she brings her parents a tray of sweet saffron buns and some coffee. She wears a white gown and a crown of greens. Her sisters and brothers dress in white and follow her. The girls carry candles and the boys wear tall, pointed caps and are called "star boys."

St. Lucia is also honored in Sicily, where she was born. Christians gather to celebrate her day with bonfires and torchlight parades. Since Lucia's name means "light," this is a very fitting way to honor St. Lucia and her faith.

Prayer: Dear God, what a strong faith You gave St. Lucia. St. Lucia truly believed in the Light of the World. Help our faith to be just as strong. Help us to shine for You, as she did. Amen.

MM#1: Celebrate St. Lucia's Day

Plan a Lucia Bride procession. Use this as an opportunity for the children in your family to honor their parents by serving them breakfast in bed. Serve Simple Saffron Buns and some non-alcoholic Glögg punch.

For St. Lucia's Day, the Swedes make saffron buns from a special sweet-roll dough. The dough is formed into an "S" shape, called Christmas pigs or boars. Double "S" buns are called Christmas goat carts. Triple "S" buns are known as Christmas wagons. This variation is a simple, quick pan roll.

Simple Saffron Buns

Yield: 10 buns   Preheat oven: 375 degrees

1 tube of refrigerator   ¼ teaspoon saffron (or
  biscuits   use 1 teaspoon ground
8 inch round cake pan   cardamom and 1 teaspoon
½ stick butter or margarine   grated orange peel)
1 tablespoon sugar   1 teaspoon cinnamon

Melt butter in cake pan. Mix spices and sprinkle in bottom of pan. Top with biscuits. Bake 8-10 minutes until golden brown. Turn out onto plate, so that spices end up on top.

Glögg

Glogg *(the o is pronounced like the ew in few)* is a warm punch that is a tradition in Scandinavian countries during the holidays. Each family has its own treasured recipe.

Yield: ten ½-cup servings

1 quart grape juice
1 10-ounce can ginger ale
1 tablespoon candied ginger
10 to 15 whole cloves
1½ teaspoon whole cardamom seed (pod discarded), slightly crushed
6 strips of orange peel, ½″ wide and 2-3″ long
3 sticks cinnamon, each 2-3″ long
⅔ cup raisins
About ¼ cup whole almonds

In glass or stainless steel bowl, combine all ingredients except raisins and almonds. Cover and let stand in refrigerator for as long as you like (as short as 15 minutes, as long as overnight). Add raisins to mixture and heat until just hot enough to sip comfortably. Do not boil. Ladle into mugs and add a few almonds.

MM#2: Invent a Word Search
Even preschoolers who can recognize letters can do word searches. What's more, they are a good way for children to practice letter recognition skills. Here's an example.
Look at the letter groups below. Circle and write every third letter. The hidden words are all things Jesus would like us to do.

AQSWEHREATYRULEFG

JHLFDOCXVDMELP

VCSMLHXCITRNZSEPT

_ _ _ _ _   _ _ _ _   _ _ _ _ _

SHARE, LOVE, SHINE

December 23 — Little Christmas Eve

Lighting the Advent Candles: We light the Prophecy Candle, the Bethlehem Candle, the Shepherds' Candle, and the Angel Candle, in remembrance of our Lord and Savior, Jesus Christ.

Hymn: "I Am So Glad Each Christmas Eve"

Scripture: John 8:12; John 9:5

Reading: Christmas Around the World

We have heard many stories and legends and customs of Christmas, from many places in the world. We have learned about crèches and *posadas, Christnacht Krippes* and *putzes.* We've heard stories about the Christmas tree and the poinsettia, holly, and rosemary. We've learned that some children hang up stockings for Christmas, while others put out their shoes.

Just as there are many different customs at Christmas, there are also different days for celebrating. In Denmark, December 23 is important. It is known as Little Christmas Eve.

A big feast is served. It includes roast goose, Christmas fish, red cabbage, and all kinds of breads and cookies. A special game is also played. An almond is hidden in the rice pudding. The person who finds it keeps this discovery a secret until everyone has finished his pudding. Then the lucky winner shows the almond and claims the prize. Usually it is candied marzipan.

The Julnisse also comes on Christmas Eve. He is a little elf, like the Swedish Jultomten. No one but the family cat ever sees him. He lives in the attic and does mischievous things.

Before they go to bed on Little Christmas Eve, the children leave the Julnisse a bowl of porridge and a pitcher of milk. By morning, they have disappeared. In their place, Julnisse leaves presents for the children.

Prayer: Dear Jesus, fill us with love this Christmas for all the people of the world. When someone looks, acts, or speaks differently than we do, we sometimes are cruel to him. We don't even try to like him. Help us to forget our differences this Christmas, dear Lord. Amen.

MM#1: Try A Scandinavian Meal. Suggested menu:
Glögg
Astrid's Swedish Meatballs
Aina's Oatmeal Crispies

Glögg

See recipe in MM#1 on St. Lucia's Day (December 13).

Astrid's Swedish Meatballs

This is a favorite family recipe, handed down from my Swedish grandmother. Our children like to help make these meatballs.

Yield: 4 servings

1 pound ground chuck
½ medium onion, minced
1 egg
½ cup bread crumbs
¼ cup rolled oats

½ teaspoon beef bouillon (or 1 cube)
¼ cup water
¼ cup sour cream
1 teaspoon salt
¼ teaspoon each: nutmeg, ginger, pepper

Dissolve bouillon in water. Mix with remaining ingredients in large bowl. Form into walnut-sized meatballs. Brown over low to medium heat. Cover and steam on low, about 35 minutes. Serve over buttered egg noodles.

Aina's Oatmeal Crispies

This is one of my mother's treasured recipes. The dough for these cookies is made ahead of time and chilled. Thus, you can make as many cookies as you have time for!

Yield: 3 dozen 3″ cookies   Preheat oven: 350 degrees

1 cup shortening	1½ cups flour
1 cup brown sugar	½ teaspoon salt
1 cup granulated sugar	1 teaspoon soda
2 eggs, well beaten	3 cups quick-cooking oats
1 teaspoon vanilla	½ cup chopped walnuts

Cream shortening and sugars. Add eggs and vanilla and beat well. Sift together flour, salt, and soda and beat into egg mixture. Add oatmeal and nuts, mixing well. Shape into rolls, about 10″ long, 3″ wide, and 1½″ tall. Wrap in waxed paper. Chill thoroughly. (Can be left in refrigerator for several days.) Slice ¼″ thick and bake on ungreased cookie sheet at 350 degrees for 10 minutes.

MM#2: Have family members reveal the names of their Special Secret Family Pals. (See Week 1, Monday.)

MM#3: Looking ahead to Christmas Day, bake a birthday cake for Jesus. Then it will be ready for Jesus' birthday party (see December 25 convocation).

December 24 — Christmas Eve

Lighting the Advent Candles: Tomorrow is Christmas Day. We have waited so long for this day. All our candles, save the Christ Candle, are now lit. Tomorrow is the birthday of our long-expected Jesus.

Hymn: "Silent Night"

Scripture: Matthew 1:18–2:12

Reading: **Stille Nacht**

America's favorite Christmas carol is "Silent Night." A man named George Gallup learned this by taking a poll. This means he called thousands of people to ask them the name of their favorite carol.

"Silent Night" was written by an Austrian pastor, Joseph Mohr. Mohr lived in the village of Oberndorf in the nineteenth century. One Christmas Eve, Mohr was preparing for worship services. Suddenly, the church organ broke down. Try as he might, Mohr could not fix the organ in time for services that evening.

He was very upset, so he went for a walk in the woods. As he walked, he talked to God, asking what he should do. Mohr kept silent, listening to God. Soon he began to feel peaceful. When he came back to the village, he sat down and wrote the words to "Silent Night," or "Stille Nacht," as it is called in German, Mohr's native language.

The beautiful music for the carol was written by Franz Gruber, the schoolmaster. He accompanied Mohr on the guitar that very Christmas Eve night.

Prayer: Dear God, thank You for the gift of music. You helped Joseph Mohr turn a frustrating situation—the broken organ—into a good one—a lovely carol telling of Jesus' birth. This carol will always remind us to keep silent and listen to what You want us to do! Amen.

MM#1: Hum "Silent Night" while sitting around the Christmas tree. Have your Advent wreath candles and the Christmas tree lights be your only source of light.

MM#2: Bake a birthday cake for Jesus if you didn't bake one yesterday.

MM#3: Reveal the names of your Special Secret Family Pals (see Week 1, Monday), if you didn't do so yesterday.

December 25—Christmas Day

Opening Words: At last Christmas is here! We have been looking forward to this day through all of Advent. Advent is past—Christmas Day is here!

But Christmas Day is a beginning—a beginning for each of us to show more love to God—and to others. May this be the start of many days when we share a smile of God's love, even with someone we don't like, when we remember to say, "I forgive you," just as God forgives us. May we think of others first, just as Jesus did when He died for us.

Hymn: "Joy to the World"

Scripture: Let us listen to the story of the coming of Jesus to earth long ago. Read Luke 2:1-20.

Lighting the Christ Candle: Today we light all the candles on our Advent wreath: the Prophecy Candle, the Bethlehem Candle, the Shepherds' Candle, the Angel Candle, and, finally, the Christ Candle. We light the Christ Candle, remembering the Light that was promised so long ago: Jesus, the Christ. All over the world, Christians are lighting candles. We share the warmth and light of our Christ Candle with them.

Reading: **A Birthday for Jesus**

(This reading follows a slightly different format than the others. In honor of this day of days, each family member will have more opportunity to participate in this convocation. The reading begins:)

Christmas was and is a gift—God giving himself to us in Jesus. Christmas is a gift I will share.

(Family members may wish to share one way they noticed that someone in their family has shared with them recently.)

Jesus has come to listen whenever I am afraid. When I am happy, He shares my joy! When I am sad, He is there to hug me!

(Family members may wish to share one way Jesus has listened to their prayers or comforted them during Advent.)

This Advent season, we have done many things to prepare for Jesus' coming. Let's share what our favorite memories are.

(Each family member can tell which thing(s) he most treasures about this Advent season.)

Prayer: Dear Jesus, thank You for preparing us for Your coming. Help us always to remember that all the Christmas cards and Christmas cookies and Christmas gifts are for celebrating Your birthday. Thank You for preparing our hearts—as well as our homes—for Your coming. Amen.

MM#1: Have Your Birthday Party for Jesus!

Sing "Happy Birthday" to Jesus and enjoy Jesus' birthday cake. For Jesus' birthday presents, have each person tell one new way he will do something Jesus would like. Some ideas are to help someone at home (dishes, bed making, etc.), find a new way to share, or try to argue less.

MM#2: Do your Puppet Play.

MM#3: Talk about continuing to meet as a family all year long. Does your family want a similar kind of devotions? Would you like to include a family night of games once a week?

Appendix

Merry Christmas the World Over

One way to foster understanding at Christmastime is to learn something about how others celebrate Jesus' birth. Use these national ways of saying "Merry Christmas" on Christmas cards, banners, or posters. Use them in your Christmas play. Feature them at your ethnic meals.

Arabia–Kol Am Wa Antom Salimeen
Belgium–Zalig Kerstfeest
Brazil–Feliz Natal
China–Tin Hoa Nian
Czechoslovakia–Vesele Vanoce
Denmark–Glaedelig Jul
England–Happy Christmas
Finland–Hauskaa Joulua
France–Joyeux Noel
Germany–Froehliche Weihnachten
Greece–Kala Chrystougena
Hungary–Kellemes Karacsonyi Unnepeket Kivanok
India–Burra Din Ki Mubarik
Ireland–Nodlaig Nait Cugat
Italy–Buon Natale
Japan–O-Medeto
Mexico–Feliz Navidad
Netherlands–Hartilijke Kerstgroeten
Norway–Gledelig Jul
Poland–Wesoloych' Swiat
Portugal–Boas Festes
Rumania–Sarbatori Vesele
Russia–S Rojolestvom Christovim
Spain–Felices Pascuas
Sweden–Gud Jul
Taiwan–Sheng Tan Kuai Loh
Wales–Nadolig Llawen
Yugoslavia–Sretan Bozich

And finally–the U. S. A.–Merry Christmas!